HOW TO GET WHATEVER YOU WANT

Top Techniques and Step-By-Step Strategies to Master the Art of Persuasion and Influence

Shaun Johnson Jr

Published by: Shaun Johnson Jr

Website: The CompleteWorksofShaunJohnsonJr.com

ISBN: 979-8-218-03716-1
Library of Congress Control Number: 2022917043
Interior Book Layout: Pixel Studio
Cover Design: Katarina
Editor: Emma Moylan

Every attempt has been made to source all quotes.

First Edition

TABLE OF CONTENTS

INTRODUCTION

Have you ever wondered how you can actually persuade or manipulate another person in order to contribute to your cause? If the answer is yes, then this book is definitely for you. The truth is that everything you have now and everything you will have in the future always comes from your interactions with other people. Therefore, consciously or unconsciously, you are always trying to persuade, manipulate and, in some cases, deceive other people through your words and actions.

Even before humanity developed the extraordinary ability to communicate verbally, the power of persuasion was of great importance and determined how our species perceived us. Of course, in those days persuasion was mostly physical, and the strongest became the dominant members of groups.

Fortunately, we have evolved and can now rely on verbal and intellectual means to try to persuade others. Part of our ability to persuade is hereditary and intuitive, but its importance is so great that it has been studied as a science for over sixty years. Eric Knowles, a professor emeritus of psychology at the University of Arkansas, explained it very well when he said, "Persuasion is a basic form of social interaction. It is the way we build consensus and common purpose."

Persuasion is used in the social, political, economic, and religious spheres, and its mastery is essential for each of us, even if we use it in different ways. In this book you will learn persuasion techniques to make people want to do what you want them to do.

Human beings are puppets, and if you know how to control their strings, you will know how to control their behavior. This book will teach you precisely how to control those strings. You will learn how to be a puppeteer in a world full of puppets.

This book contains the most comprehensive techniques of human psychology, persuasion and manipulation to help you achieve your personal goals. It is perfect for anyone who wants to improve their interactions with their environment.

In the first chapters you will learn the basic concepts of human psychology, persuasion and manipulation. Then you will learn the basic methods of conditioning and persuasion. Later you will learn how to determine people's motivations. Mastering this knowledge will be like taking control of the strings of a puppet. Next, you will learn how to persuade people without expressing an argument. After that you will learn an effective step-by-step persuasion procedure. Once you have gained this practical knowledge, we will delve into the principles of persuasion, techniques and professional formulas to increase your power of persuasion. We will also take a look at persuasion through language patterns, the art of persuasive writing, and a dangerous manipulation technique.

Most of the techniques in this book exert an "unconscious" influence, which means that people will not know that these principles guide their behavior.

I hope you like it.

Comment: Throughout the book I will use the term *subject* to refer to the person or people you are trying to persuade. I will also use the term *request* when trying to persuade someone to take an action.

ACKNOWLEDGMENTS

This book is dedicated to the Creator, my ancestors, my mother, my family, and friends. A special thanks to LaLa for being a pillar of support during this journey.

To the brothers of my fraternity who continue to inspire me to be a better man ... THANK YOU!

CHAPTER 1:

WHAT IS PERSUASION?

"The best skill in life is to get along with others and influence their actions." – John Hancock

Persuasion is "an interactive process by which a given message alters an individual's perspective by changing the knowledge, beliefs, or interests underlying that perspective" (Miller, 1980). In other words, persuasion is communication that influences or induces other people to change their thoughts, feelings, desires and behaviors.

Persuasion operates in such a manner that the subject is presented with information in a way that requires a reexamination of personal values and beliefs in a different light. The person thus enters into a gradual process of changing their internal and external attitudes. Therein lies the paradox of influence. The determinations and restrictions of free will are not imposed from outside, but **proposed**.

We perform numerous actions automatically, in a stereotypical way. No matter what the reasons, the fact is that these behavior patterns easily bring us under the influence of persuasive or manipulative individuals. According to psychologists Petty and Cacioppo's model of persuasion, known as the elaboration likelihood method (ELM), there are two processing paths when a person is presented with new information: the central path and the peripheral path.

The central path refers to knowledge. A person receives new information, accompanied by strong or weak arguments, which he or she then analyzes in light of previous knowledge. The result is an acceptance or rejection of the proposed message, while the changes it produces in the argument are of a lasting nature. Important factors in this process are cognition, motivation and interest. For this reason, arguments must first be rational, with demonstrations of causation according to the cause-and-effect principle, and then accompanied by a practical explanation of how to achieve the desired goals.

Based on this information, it has been found through experiments that the request for a favor is more easily answered when a reason (a motivation) is provided. Providing a reason helps people freely decide what to do. Even a very simple explanation can lead to a positive response.

The peripheral path, on the other hand, refers to noncognitive aspects, such as time and space, emotions, credibility, character, and senses involved in perception. The quality of arguments is secondary, while the influence and changes produced are proportionately less stable and less lasting. This method is widely used in the world of advertising. It works through stimulation of emotions, personal liking, sense of leadership, humor, physical attraction and many other modalities. The central and peripheral pathways are not mutually exclusive. They can work well together in order to make us more persuasive.

At this point, it is important to understand how there is a big difference between persuasion and manipulation. It is perfectly possible to manipulate people into doing something they may not want to do, but in the long run they will notice, they will become angry, and the result will reduce your ability to persuade that person later. A classic example of this comes from pressure selling techniques in which customers are forced to buy a product or service they do not want or need. Ideally, persuasion is most effective when you lead a person to something you both want, even if the end result is more beneficial to you than to the other person. The fact that you both benefited, even if not equally, means that the source of resentment has been eliminated.

Too many people confuse manipulation with persuasion – you need to understand that they are completely different. Manipulation is the act of forcing a person to do something he or she does not want to do. Persuasion, on the other hand, is an art. It is the art of getting a person to do something that is in your interest, but is also in agreement with his or her interest.

The main difference between persuasion and manipulation lies in the intention. A person who tries to be persuasive sincerely believes that they are working in the best interest of both. A manipulator cares only about their own benefits and may persuade others to do something that is not good for them or even harmful. Persuasion also includes some sincerity and transparency in the process, factors absent or obscured in manipulation. The difference is similarly visible in the net benefit or impact on the other person. Persuasion aims at the will of the other person. It is about making others want to do what you want them to do. We have to work with the needs of the other person. And there is no obligation to invent new needs. Nature has provided us with enough of them. In most cases, it will be enough to stimulate an existing need, and the other person will spontaneously follow the path we have laid out for him or her. Therefore, it is useful to know about human needs.

There are basic needs such as food, drink, air, sleep, health, and sex. We also have a need for goods expressed in money and all that this can buy. Also of great importance are emotional and intellectual needs with their aspects of growth and maturity, social and personal impacts, pleasure and happiness.

According to renowned psychologist Abraham Maslow, human needs can be structured in a pyramidal hierarchy. At the base of the pyramid are physiological needs such as air, food, water, sex, and survival. One level above we find security needs such as physical security, employment, resources, family health and property. One step higher are the needs related to love and belonging, friendship and family. Going up further we find esteem needs, such as trust, achievement, respect for others, and respect by others. Finally, self-actualization, morality, creativity, spontaneity, lack of prejudice, and acceptance of facts are at the top of the pyramid. In his later days, Abraham Maslow spoke of an extra dimension of human needs, in which the individual transcends to higher goals of altruism and spirituality. We will go into more detail in a later section, as it is necessary to understand this well in order to be effective in persuading others.

CHAPTER 2:

BASIC METHODS OF CONDITIONING, PERSUASION AND MANIPULATION

"If you can't get people to listen to your ideas, tell them it's confidential."
– Anonymous

In the course of the years, various experts and persuaders have developed methods that can be used to guide the thinking of individuals or groups of people. Below we outline four methods to help you develop your strategy.

Reward-punishment system

The simplest and most identifiable technique revolves around reward and punishment. With this method, it is possible to influence others to achieve a desired outcome. Unlike many other techniques, this one has short- and long-term effects.

The principle behind this concept may seem very simple, but it must be used carefully. In essence, it rewards any positive act and punishes any negative act. For example, one of your employees completes his or her projects effectively and efficiently within the set time frame. Since this is the positive behavior you desire, you will reinforce this action by providing your employee with an effective and valuable reward. It must be a reward for your employee, so choose something they will appreciate.

When the case is the opposite of that presented above and your employee submits late and sloppy work, you should apply punishment to discourage such behavior. However, as with rewards, it must be proportionate. Too severe a punishment will discourage anyone. Too lenient, and your employee will learn nothing; on the contrary, it will be like reinforcement for their unacceptable actions. You might ask them to stay a while outside working hours to make corrections.

It is very easy to use this system inappropriately. An effective reward-punishment system is based on each person's individual likes and dislikes. It uses quick and simple reward or punishment actions. By immediately showing a positive or negative action, you encourage or discourage repetition of an action. That said, don't show your cards for all to see. The lessons you impart must be silent; otherwise, they will not be effective. This is a very effective method of gaining immediate and future benefits.

Classical air-conditioning system

This technique is a bit more complicated to use than the previous one, but it is very effective. Classical conditioning finds its roots in Russia with Ivan Pavlov. Pavlov conducted a behavioral conditioning experiment with his dogs. In this experiment, food was given to the dogs after ringing a bell. Once the dogs were accustomed to this routine, they began drooling as soon as the bell rang, even if they were not presented with food. Pavlov had conditioned his dogs to react in the way he desired by using positive reinforcement and lateral association.

This experiment established how we can associate a positive attribute with certain actions to achieve the desired result. For example, imagine you are the parent of an exuberant child. You might want them to calm down at certain times without having to tell them in an angry way. You can choose a single gesture, three hand claps, a hand motion, or a finger in their mouth, and repeat that gesture each time you ask them to calm down. After some time, begin to stop the verbal commands and use only the gesture as a command. Over time, the child will begin to associate the gesture with the desired outcome.

The beauty of this type of conditioning is how subtle and natural it can be. However, it cannot be used everywhere and does not have immediate results. Nevertheless, it is a powerful method to consider.

Reaction method

This is a very simple method that we all use on a daily basis. It works well in the short and long term, but requires the use of appropriate language. This method does not require any association or a reward-punishment system. Rather, you simply tell the other person that you want a certain reaction from him or her. This is a direct approach, but it works in many situations. For example, you can tell your partner that you need them to do the dishes because you do not have time. Again, you do not need to associate this action with any reward; verbal recognition is sufficient. However, make sure you do not appear desperate or pressurize.

The need to be a special model

This method is based on our basic need to be considered special by those around us. Most human beings like to feel how different and unique they are. This feeds our need for acceptance and helps us recognize our positive actions. So with this method, you start by praising the individual from whom you want to get a reaction. You will tell them how special they are and how much they mean to you. Then you will explain how the desired act will make you maintain a positive opinion of them. Do this in a subtle way. In many cases, the need to be special will make people want to exceed expectations and do better. In leadership strategies it is said that you should give people a reputation they want to maintain. The key is to recognize and show appreciation for certain characteristics (real or not) of the person, so that they themselves will strive to maintain that special reputation.

These four methods can be used to influence the behavior of almost any person.

CHAPTER 3:
WHAT MOTIVATES US

Every day, personality tests are posted on Facebook that show which TV character we resemble. It's fun to see which Disney character you are, but that doesn't mean anything, and these tests certainly don't help.

Before continuing, I should clarify that when I talk about personality I am talking about the essence of the person and not about learned behavior. Later we will talk about "behavioral masks."

In real life there are four basic personality types that help us find out what motivates and what frustrates people. The good news is that people don't need to take personality tests as if they were applying for a new job. You just have to answer two questions:

- Is the person primarily hesitant or impulsive?
- Is the person primarily an extrovert or introvert?

Let's see how to answer the first question:

Shy people are quiet, slow and very indirect. They speak slowly and think cautiously. They move carefully and express themselves cautiously. They prefer questions. They hesitate before acting. They have an enormous inner need to get **things right**. They tend to move away from consequences rather than toward their goals.

Impulsive people are quick and very direct. They talk fast and move quickly. They think quickly and act impulsively. They express themselves easily and directly. They have an enormous internal need to get **things done**. They tend to move toward their goals and do not worry about consequences.

Now let's see how to answer the second question:

Extroverted people tend to be immediately friendly with everyone. They tell stories easily and spontaneously, share secrets and express their emotions, because they believe that doing so brings them closer to people. Extroverts are people oriented and externally supported. They often make decisions based on the emotions and opinions of others. They are very affective and demonstrative in their relationships. They are naturally interested in the opinions and emotions of others.

Introverts tend to be goal oriented and internally recognized. They also tell stories, share secrets, and express their emotions, but only if there is a good reason to do so. Introverts open up only when they believe that sharing their emotions, stories, and secrets will bring them closer to what they want. They can be very affectionate, but they tend to limit their affections to selected people they care about. They like to base decisions on their own logic and inner understanding, rather than worrying about the opinions and emotions of others.

Use this information to identify the personality types of your friends and family members. Each personality type deals with life differently, so knowing this information will make it easier for you to make persuasive approaches.

It is easier to understand the combinations of the four personality types if you outline them on paper. Draw a horizontal line and on the far left write "mostly hesitant" and on the far right write "mostly impulsive." Now draw a vertical line that crosses the horizontal line you just drew in the middle. At the top write "mostly extroverted" and at the bottom write "mostly introverted." At this point you will have four quadrants.

Try to classify people close to you into one of these quadrants. In the following sections we will examine each personality type in detail to find out what motivates and frustrates them.

Who is an intuitive?

People in the "mostly extrovert-mostly impulsive" quadrant are called intuitive. They are also called socializers. They believe that life should be fun. They are people oriented and goal oriented.

Intuitive personalities believe that their main purpose is to enjoy life. They tend to perform impulsive acts of kindness, impulsive acts of friendship and impulsive acts of any kind. They love to talk. They like to be the center of attention. They are enthusiastic by nature.

On the other hand, they must learn to control their impulsiveness, or they will often set themselves up for failure or make commitments that they cannot keep.

Intuitives do not care about logic and are bad with details. They are capable of doing detailed and logical work, but prefer not to do it. They are surprised when their debts come due each month. They tend to think, "Haven't I already paid them?"

If you have ever asked yourself, "How did I get into this situation," you are probably an intuitive person, but the real test of whether or not you are an intuitive person is to ask yourself what bothers you most.

What bothers intuitive people the most? Routine, structure, and especially any person who highlights their "illogical" behavior and expects to change their way of being.

Remember that they live for approval. When dealing with intuitive personalities, be dynamic and appreciative. Help them focus on one thing at a time, and always show them attention and approval. They will love your efforts and reward you with enthusiasm and energy.

Who is a doer?

People in the "primarily introverted-primarily impulsive" quadrant are called doers. They are also called directors. They live to have a purpose.

Doer personalities feel that the main purpose of life is to achieve something meaningful. They live to see the contributions made by them to the world. They tend to be goal oriented and future oriented. They love to be part of something big and important. They want to leave a mark on the world. They feel good when they achieve a goal and dislike people who get in their way.

When doer personalities feel trapped by people or circumstances, they become irritable and abrupt. When they hear others talking, their minds begin to wander. They just want people to get to the point without deviation.

Doer personalities live to achieve goals, but they must understand that not everyone lives the same way they do.

If you've ever asked yourself, "Why don't you just get to the point and leave me alone?" you're probably a doer. But, again, the real test of whether you are a doer is to ask yourself what bothers you most.

What bothers a doer? The waiting, the hesitation, and the waste of time.

In fact, doers must control their own choices and destiny. When dealing with doers, you must always be concise, get to the point, help them discover solutions, give them alternatives, help them achieve their goals, give them credit for their achievements, and don't waste their time. If you give them the control they need, they will love you and become your best employees.

Who is a thinker?

People in the "mostly introverted-mostly tentative" quadrant are called thinkers. They are also known as intellectuals and thrive when things make sense.

Thinking personalities believe that the main purpose of existence is to understand the patterns that make life possible. They love to know the *why* and the *how*. They navigate through the facts of life and try to make sense of things. They like structure, predictability, numbers, the scientific method, evidence and physical proof. They appreciate logical discussion and are uncomfortable with emotional excess.

Thinking personalities are perfectionists. They want the world to make perfect sense, and they have a hard time accepting that not everyone cares as much about logic and precision as they do. It does not seem logical to them that some people can operate without logic.

Thinkers want to correct illogical thinking, even when the illogical thinking comes from someone else.

When people do not cooperate with them by giving them the rationale they require, thinkers feel unstable and often walk away from the situation.

Thinking personalities spend a lot of energy trying to make sense of problematic life events so that they can tend to avoid such events in the future.

When they encounter a difficulty, they want to investigate the exact cause of their frustration and often review each event in sequence to discover the problem.

They need to understand that not everyone cares about things making sense and being logical.

If you've ever asked yourself, "Don't you see that it doesn't make sense?" you're probably a thinker. Again, the real test of whether you are a thinker is when you ask yourself what bothers you most.

What bothers a thinker? Inaccuracy, lack of planning, forcing and impulsive actions, bad advice, and illogical behavior.

When dealing with thinkers, one must be precise, thorough, organized and methodical. Appreciate their logic and deep understanding of things. Give them time. They need time to do good work, but not indefinite time. Their deep need to get things done right often means they never feel ready. So help them create deadlines. And help them see how illogical it is to always expect logic and perfection in others. They will appreciate your understanding and become the best possible collaborator.

Who is a sensitive?

People in the "mostly extrovert-mostly uncertain" quadrant are called sensitive. They are also called speakers and live for their relationships.

Sensitive personalities believe that the main purpose of life is to build deep and sincere relationships with other people. They tend to be good listeners. They also usually care a lot about what other people think and feel. They are happiest when everyone around them is happy, so they do their best to contribute to the happiness of others. They love to communicate their feelings and emotions. They like to approach people and help them find containment. Sensitive people are cooperative, balanced, friendly, sensitive, concerned and talkative. They are the amalgam that holds the group together, and they work tirelessly to have harmonious relationships.

On the other hand, they are very uncomfortable with any behavior that threatens the stability and harmony of their relationships. They are easily hurt when they see themselves as victims of insensitive behavior, and rather than make a scene, they keep the hurt inside.

They tend to develop resentments and become overwhelmed or disillusioned by the behavior of others. They often think, "Why can't people be nicer?"

When they stop taking every action themselves and stop expecting everyone to be as sensitive as they are, they can find great balance in their lives.

If you have ever asked yourself, "Why is this person so cruel?" you are probably a sensitive person. Again, the real test of whether you are a sensitive person is to ask yourself what bothers you most.

What bothers a sensitive person? People or situations that are abrupt, rough, unpredictable, quarrelsome, any action that threatens the peace and harmony of one's day.

When dealing with sensitive people you must be friendly, empathetic, patient, cooperative, accepting and give them your time. They will thrive under your support and become a base of support in your life.

A few words about behavioral masks

We cannot go on without talking about behavioral masks. As I said before, behavioral masks are different from personality. Personality is intrinsic to the person. We could say that the person is born with personality. In contrast, behavioral masks are a learned behavior throughout life.

This can be appreciated in kindergarten children. You can find the intuitive or sociable ones running around, playing, and seeking approval. You can find the doers or directors playing with other children only if they are willing to play in their own way. You can notice the thinkers or intellectuals as they sit around thinking about how the big clock on the wall works. And you'll be able to see the sensitive ones, or speakers, as they seek harmonious relationships and play with other children, but when things get complicated they get uncomfortable and scared.

All these children, however, will over time develop something called a behavioral mask. These are behaviors they have learned in order to relate to others. Let's take sensitive children as an example. We have already seen that they seek relationships in harmony, acceptance and stability. They do not like to lose control, but what happens when a sensitive child grows up in an unstable home where the only way to achieve stability is to behave like a doer? The sensitive personality in their quest for stability will begin to behave more impulsively, more introverted, they may even begin to control relationships, but deep down they will not be interested in control, but in the harmony of relationships.

What about a doer? We have seen that they like to lead, hate waiting, desire appreciation, recognition, and control, but being introverted they will probably have few friends. When a doer realizes that the only way to gain appreciation and recognition is through friends, they may begin to behave like a sensitive person. They will learn to be more talkative, show interest in people, and build decent relationships.

It is important to note that masks of behavior can go both ways. For example, sensitives can become more impulsive or more introverted depending on their environment and the basic motivations they want to fulfill. In other words, we are always able to change our behavior as we age, but our original motivations remain the same.

How to interact effectively with the four personality types

Intuitive:

They are: Outgoing and impulsive.

They want: To live for fun.

Desire: Approval, attention and recognition.

Their behavior is: Dynamic, alive and exciting.

They get annoyed by: Routine and organization.

Their strengths are: Creating enthusiasm and motivating others.

Their weaknesses are: Disorganization and disapproval. They often make impulsive promises and then forget them. They find it unnatural to plan their lives. They are also easily overwhelmed and feel threatened when they are the object of disapproval.

They are afraid: Of being rejected.

Likes: Encouraging people.

In a game they are: Spontaneous.

In discussions they are: Playful, dramatic and funny.

They decide: Impulsively. They tend to make decisions based on their intuition and what they feel is right at the time.

Under stress: They become sarcastic.

They support: Their ideas.

They focus on: Interactions.

To persuade: They provide incentives and testimonials.

When they are emotional: They become impulsive, demanding and sarcastic.

Executors:

They are: Introverted and impulsive.

They want to: Control their own destiny.

Desire: Appreciation, recognition and fulfillment.

Their behavior is: Fast, instinctive and independent.

They get annoyed by: Waiting and indecision.

Their strengths are: Making decisions and completing goals.

Their weaknesses are: Impatience. They become abrupt and irritated when people or circumstances come between them and their goals. They may appear thoughtless, careless or aggressive when they feel blocked by others.

They are afraid: Of being manipulated.

Likes: People who get to the point and don't waste time.

In a game they are: Competitive.

In discussions they are: Concise, concise and precise.

They decide: Independently. They hate being told what to do and need choices and control over all potential options.

Under stress: They are abrupt and dictatorial.

They support: Their own goals.

They focus on: Results.

To persuade: They provide options with analysis.

When they are emotional: They become critical and uncooperative.

Thinkers:

They are: Introverted and shy.

They want: For life to have meaning.

Desire: Accuracy, order and precision.

Their behavior is: Precise, logical and unemotional.

They get annoyed by: Illogical people.

Their strengths are: They analyze relationships, situations and data.

Their weaknesses are: Perfectionism, indecision, and procrastination. They hate making mistakes, so they often wait until the last minute to act. They are also extremely intolerant of the impulsive and illogical actions of others.

They are afraid: Of making mistakes.

Likes: That people are accurate.

In a game they are: Structured.

In discussions they are: Realistic, organized and accurate.

Deciding: Deliberating. They gather, analyze and evaluate all the facts, and then choose the most logical option.

Under stress: They withdraw from the situation.

They support: Their procedures.

They focus on: Processes.

To persuade: They provide data and documentation.

When they are emotional: They feel hurt, worried, confused and isolated.

Sensitive:

They are: Outgoing and shy.

They want: People to get along with.

Desire: Harmony, acceptance and stability.

Their behavior is: Kind, friendly and concerned.

They get annoyed by: Insensitive people.

Their strengths are: Listening and relating to people.

Their weaknesses are: Hesitation and sensitivity. They are likely to hold grudges and be influenced by past wounds. They are often concerned with how they influence people rather than how people influence them.

They are afraid: Of any sudden change.

Likes: That people feel comfortable.

In a game they are: Friendly, political and talkative.

In discussions they are: Disengaged.

They decide: Consulting. They need the opinion of others and want to know how their decisions will affect others.

Under stress: They are submissive and flexible.

They support: Their feelings.

They focus on: Communication.

To persuade: They provide some personal guarantees.

When they are emotional: They are uncertain, calm and dismissive.

The seven universal motivators

Regardless of personality influence, we must recognize that human beings share some basic motivators. I now present the seven universal motivators. These seven motivators can make people "buy into" your ideas.

Note: When I talk about buying, I do so in its most generic form. When we want to convince someone of our point of view, what we really want to do is sell them our ideas.

1. Desire for profit

The desire for profit is usually expressed in financial terms. We all want extra money to feel safe. We also want some extra money to have fun.

The desire for profit is why we buy stocks, work, hire employees, educate ourselves and invest in companies.

2. Fear of losing

The fear of losing is also mostly financial in nature. We work very hard to get what we have and do not want to lose it. The fear of losing explains why we do not take advantage of certain good opportunities.

3. Comfort and convenience

We all like comfort and convenience. That's why there are people who take charge of picking up our trash, washing our car, and taking care of our garden. We are willing to pay someone else to do those little things we don't like so that we can feel more comfortable.

Convenience and convenience explain why we buy microwave ovens and washing machines.

4. Safety and security

Safety and security usually involve protecting our loved ones. Security explains why we take out life insurance, even though we will not be alive to benefit from it. We buy anything to protect our loved ones.

5. Pride of ownership

We believe our possessions tell something about us, so we want to make sure they say the right things. Pride of ownership is what drives us to buy a stolen painting for our private collection, to buy a sweater worn by Marilyn Monroe, a sports car or pay thousands of dollars for a pair of shoes.

6. Satisfaction of emotion

We buy cards, gifts, dinners and movie tickets in an attempt to win someone else's love, admiration or forgiveness. Also to show our emotions of love, admiration, acceptance and forgiveness.

7. Ego satisfaction

We like to treat ourselves well. We like to look good. Ego satisfaction makes us buy makeup, go to the gym, have cosmetic surgery, buy expensive perfumes and have our picture taken at an exclusive resort.

These seven motivators are used by professional marketers and advertising agencies to get us to buy their products. You can use these same tools to motivate others to approve your ideas or hire your talents.

The point is as follows. If you tell people why you want or need them to do something, you will only get the reputation of someone who is desperate. However, if you show people how your ideas and talents will bring them money, protection, comfort, security, pride, love, or any of the other reasons we have already seen, those same people will begin to appreciate your perspective.

When people appreciate your point of view, you are a persuasive person.

Maslow's hierarchy of needs

Let me introduce you to another tool that will enable you to understand what motivates and convinces people. This is Maslow's hierarchy of needs.

Here's how it works.

Survival

The first need in the pyramid is survival. People are willing to do anything to survive. They work in places they hate. They commit crimes. They betray their friends. They betray themselves. They get involved with people they are not normally interested in. When their survival is threatened, they will do anything to get out unscathed. Once survival is assured, we develop a desire to satisfy the second need in Maslow's hierarchy.

Security

Security means that we know that we will survive not only today but also tomorrow, next week, next year, and the next generation. We need to ensure our ability to survive the challenges of tomorrow. The essential need for security is what makes people so afraid of change. When security is threatened in any way, such as a change in the near future, people are strongly motivated to restore it. Once our future is secure, the third need in Maslow's hierarchy will appear.

Enrollment

Belonging is fulfilled when we connect with a community. The community could be work, family or neighborhood. We enjoy being part of a community. We like working with people who understand us, are friendly, laugh at our jokes and share our values. On the other hand, our sense of belonging feels threatened when we look around at our work, our community, our family or our friends, and for some reason we know we don't fit into that environment. We start to feel that we don't belong, and if we can't satisfy that need, we will start looking for another place to belong. When we have satisfied the need to belong, the next need in Maslow's hierarchy appears.

Prestige

The need for prestige is satisfied when we feel recognized for what we give to the community to which we belong. Whenever we feel appreciated, respected and recognized by the group to which we belong, our need for prestige is satisfied. But if our need for prestige is not satisfied, we will begin to wonder why we work so hard for nothing. We will begin to wonder why we bother. We will hesitate to make every extra effort that our community requires. We will begin to move away and look for a better place to ensure our survival and belonging. However, if our need for prestige is continuously met by our community, the fifth and final need in Maslow's hierarchy will appear.

Self-realization

Self-actualization means that we know that our growth is assured. We know that we are on our way to becoming a better version of ourselves. We know that we are on the path to success and that the people around us support our success. We see our future expanding. We like to see who we are becoming. If this last need is not met, people will never be truly fulfilled. When you prevent people from getting better, or even if they just suspect that you are preventing them from getting better, they will begin to see you as an obstacle in their path and look for ways to leave you behind. However, if you show that their growth and self-fulfillment are assured, they will remain totally loyal.

Now that you know how the hierarchy of needs works, how can you use this information to improve your ability to persuade? Think about it:

What happens if one of the needs in Maslow's hierarchy is not met?

What if the person you are trying to convince doubts their own confidence?

What if something were to happen to make you doubt your security, such as losing your job or a relationship?

If your need for survival was not met, would you worry about the need for belonging?

What happens if someone feels that their ideas and ideals are not being recognized? The answer is simple: they will look elsewhere.

In short, it is essential to understand where people are in this matrix of hierarchies to know what motivates and convinces them.

CHAPTER 4:

HOW TO GET SOMEONE TO AGREE WITH YOU

The secret of Socrates

How do you get someone to agree with you?

Two thousand years ago, Socrates had already discovered this secret. Questions are the key to persuasion. If you want to be truly persuasive, you must learn to ask more and give fewer instructions. **In other words, never give instructions if you can ask a question**.

For example:

Don't tell people what to think; ask them what they think.

Don't tell people what to do; rather, ask what they want from life and how they plan to get it.

Don't insist on making people listen to you; ask them attention-grabbing questions.

Don't tell people they need to change; ask them what will happen if they continue with their current behavior.

Don't expect people to think differently; rather, ask them questions that stimulate their thoughts.

Of course, if you ask too many questions at the wrong time, people will become suspicious of your motives. They may even get angry because you are meddling in their business. But if you learn to ask the right questions at the right time, you will learn to open people's hearts. Also, once you start asking effective questions, you will begin to overcome the biggest barrier in human communication: attention span.

The human attention span is about twenty seconds, so unless they are really interested in what you have to say, other people's minds will quickly begin to digress. If you want to capture and hold people's attention, you need to talk about topics that interest them. And, once again, questions are key.

After all, you cannot count on people being interested in your words, but you can count on someone being interested in their answers.

In the next lesson you will learn three types of questions to always have in your arsenal to be truly convincing.

Three types of questions

There are three types of questions that can improve your persuasion skills. These are: open-ended questions, closed questions and confirmation questions.

Open-ended questions

Open-ended questions usually begin with who, what, when, where, how or why.

This includes all questions that cannot be answered with a yes or no. Asking good open-ended questions will help you gather information about problems, opinions, feelings, motivations, people, and circumstances, so think strategically.

Closed questions

Closed questions are always answered with yes or no.

They usually begin with phrases such as would you, can you, are you, and will you? These questions are used to establish areas of consensus, confirm understanding, restore attention, or make introductions.

Confirmation questions

Confirmation questions are a form of closed question. They confirm that you are paying attention and that you really understand what the other person is saying.

With confirmation questions you simply repeat what you think the person is saying, and then ask if you have interpreted the message correctly. If used correctly, confirmation questions demonstrate a sincere desire to communicate, but if used incorrectly they will make you sound like a manipulative person or an annoying parrot.

The key word is sincerity.

When used together, these three types of questions will help you establish the areas of consent that you will use later.

A typical combination of questions looks like this:

"You want more *money*, right? If I can make you more *money*, will you listen to me?"

Replace the word *money* with any motivator you have discovered and see the effect it has.

"You want more fun, right? If I can show you how to have more fun, will you give my suggestions a chance?"

"You want your children to respect you, don't you? If I can show you how to get that respect, will you do something for me?"

In essence, persuasion is about showing others how to get what they want by choosing the path you suggest.

Whether you try to give orders or win with arguments, people will tend to build barriers against you. However, when you ask questions, you are making agreements and making suggestions based on your sincere understanding, so people will tend to appreciate and remain open to your opinion.

When you give orders instead, you are asking for trouble. You should never tell people what to do. Instead, learn to ask questions and offer choices.

CHAPTER 5:

STEP-BY-STEP PERSUASION PROCEDURE

In this section we will look at a step-by-step persuasion procedure. This is a basic but very effective persuasion method that puts into practice what you have learned so far. As you practice it and adapt it to your style, you should supplement it with the more advanced knowledge and concepts that I will teach you throughout the book.

The approach

To build trust, you have to be a person who can be trusted. In other words, you have to become an honest, caring and conscientious person.

Being an honest person means being sincere, consistent, tending to honor and keep promises.

Being a caring person means caring about the opinions, happiness and success of others.

Finally, being a conscientious person means being able to recognize cause and effect, possessing good judgment, and being able to understand and design creative solutions to problems.

Thoughtful and perceptive people earn people's trust.

Also be sure to draw positive attention to yourself. In other words, don't start talking if people are not open to your words.

I have seen couples hold entire conversations while one person watched TV. I've even seen parents trying to have an important conversation with their children already at the door, ready to leave. You should learn to ask for a few minutes of people's attention before you start talking, or you will spend most of your time talking to yourself.

Ask, "Do you have time to talk about something important?" or even better, "When would be a good time to ask you about something important?"

Finally, keep calm. When people become emotional, you should simply listen to them and provide sympathetic responses. Do not try to reason with an illogical person.

Remember that when people are open to logic, they usually demand it. Most importantly, when you begin to enter an emotional state, you must recognize your emotions immediately. We become emotional when people cross our boundaries or when they contradict our definitions. Try saying something like, "You've given me a lot to think about, so let's continue the discussion another time." If you try to reach an agreement while you are emotionally involved, both sides will regret it.

Questions

Once you have established trust and a proper level of focus, you can move on to questions. At this point one of the first questions you should ask is:

"To understand the situation better, may I ask a few questions?"

In other words, ask your interlocutor's permission before you start asking questions.

Be sure to listen for answers using all the tools at your disposal.

Body language: Do they seem uncomfortable? Are there signs that they are lying? For more details on how to read body language you can read my book *How to Detect Lies Using Body Language*.

Emotion: Remember that emotional people are harder to convince.

Reflection: What do your words say about your belief system?

Meaning: Do you and the other person use the same definitions?

Paraphrase: May I repeat your words and confirm that I understand your point of view?

In general, don't get frustrated if you can't persuade someone who is unwilling to hear what you have to say. Your goal is to keep the subject's attention and to use questions to understand the needs, wants, and motivations of the person you want to persuade. Remember that you cannot influence situations that you do not understand.

At this stage try to use open-ended questions. This way you can get the subject's attention and gain information to improve your own understanding. Ask questions that begin with who, when, where, and how. Switch to closed questions and confirmation questions only when you are ready to confirm your understanding of the situation.

Keep asking questions until you feel confident you understand the situation and can avoid saying things the person already knows, or you will lose attention. People are always telling smokers to stop smoking, people who want to lose weight are told to stop eating, and delinquents are told to stop committing crimes. Smokers, dieters, and offenders are usually aware of the consequences of what they are doing, so do you really think that communicating to them what they already know will make a difference?

Before you start telling people what you know, you should try asking what they know. You will be surprised to find that the people you are trying to counsel know their situation better than you do.

You can also use your questions to help people see the difference between an easy choice and a convenient one. Many people have difficulty making decisions and fulfilling commitments because they cannot decide between two things that are good or bad. You can use your questions to help them discover the emotional mazes that prevent them from taking action.

Makeup:

As we have seen, we tend to think that persuasion occurs when one person does something for another, but the truth is that science has shown that people do things for themselves. Your goal is to peel back all the superficial layers of a person to find the real reasons why they will do something: by asking the right questions you can find out the truth.

Let's examine a hypothetical case. Suppose you are the father of a teenage daughter and her room is a mess. You want your daughter to clean her room; how do you go about it?

You can try to force her by imposing your authority, you can try to threaten her, you can talk to her about the meaning of a clean room ... This may work in the short term, but now I will teach you a very effective persuasion technique called motivational interviewing.

This technique consists of asking two irrational questions. Suppose your daughter's name is Mary; the two questions you will ask are as follows:

"Mary, on a scale of one to ten, where one means you are not ready and ten means you are ready to do it now, how ready are you to clean your room?"

Now, Maria's room looks like a mess, so she won't give you a ten or a nine, or even a five.

She will say, "Dad, I'm a two."

At this point our instincts would make us say, "Why a two? It should be a nine!" Here you will ask the second question, which is really interesting and contradictory. You will answer, "OK, Maria, you are a two. Why didn't you choose a lower number?"

Now, Mary will be confused because this question has overridden all the defenses she had put up. Now she has to think and explain why she didn't choose a one. She will probably answer, "Well, Dad, I have to clean and tidy up my room so I can get dressed faster in the morning and not be late for school, and maybe meet my friends in the afternoon."

What happened here? With the second question Mary began to articulate her own reasons for doing something. And this is the key to persuasion, which is for the person to discover their own reasons for doing something.

Now, suppose Maria says she is a one. In this case things are a little more complicated, but it is important that you understand this. You will answer, "Maria, what can we do to make you a two?" Maria might respond, "Well, if you would give me fifteen minutes to spare, that would be a great help to get me started. Maybe if I didn't have to set the table every night, or if I didn't have to take out the trash, I would have a little more time to myself." Usually when people are a one, it is not because they are stubborn, but because they have some obstacle in their environment. So when someone answers that they are a one, find out what the obstacle is and try to solve it so that they are a two.

This technique can be used universally. Remember, the key to persuasion is to find reasons why people would do something.

Agree on the necessity

"The only way to influence others is to talk about what they want and show them how to get it." – Dale Carnegie

Once you have taken the time to find out the motivations of the person you are trying to persuade, you need to confirm, clarify, and agree on the desired outcome. If you want to be truly persuasive, the desired outcome must be something the other person wants as much as you do. This is the step where you will use confirmation questions to establish areas of agreement.

An example might be, "So if I get this, you want ___________. Correct?"

At this stage you seek agreement on something that needs to be done. It is necessary to actively search for areas of agreement. Unless you successfully complete this step and accept that there is a need, you are very unlikely to persuade anyone.

Try to agree on principles, not positions. Position arguments are used to decide who is right and who is wrong. Don't waste your time trying to get someone to admit that they are wrong. Instead, look for principles on which both sides agree.

For example, "In principle, it doesn't matter who is right and who is wrong, because what we need is to solve this situation, right?"

Please note that we use a closed question designed to get a "yes," and when you get that "yes" you can move on to the next point.

Authority

This step is widely used in sales. It consists of giving an explanation of your authority in 150 words or less (known as an elevator speech). One hundred and fifty words or less is an important parameter; remember that the human attention span is limited.

In your personal life you might skip this step, since the person you are trying to persuade certainly knows your authority. Although it would not be out of place to remind them.

Statements of authority should be about facts.

For example:

"I represent a company founded in 1975. During that time we have helped more than fourteen million people lower their operating costs. We also have five stars on the Fortune 400 list, just to give you an idea."

The statement of authority simply shows that they can trust you in that you really know what you are talking about. Once the other person is clear about your authority, you can move on to the next step: making your presentation.

Submit your solution

When you have a solution to propose:

First of all, expose it.

Second, describe its benefits by creating a clear picture of the needs it meets.

Third, ask the subject if he or she agrees that it is worth trying.

This technique in sales is called features, benefit and reaction. It is an extremely effective persuasion tool.

For example, suppose I want you to buy one of my books. First, I name a feature of my book (teaches persuasion step by step). Then, I describe in vivid detail the facts about that feature. I remind you of the last time you tried to persuade someone with your arguments. I will ask you how much energy you expended and how much frustration it generated. Finally, I will ask you if your arguments produced the effect you wanted.

If you are not satisfied with the effect of your arguments, I will ask, "Do you want to learn how to reach agreements without arguing?" That way I will have your reaction to my proposal.

Here are a few more examples of the technique's characteristics, benefit and reaction.

Example 1

Feature: You can learn the different personality types and what motivates each one.

Advantages: It can save you time and frustration, making you more persuasive.

Response: Is there someone in your life you would like to persuade or motivate?

Example 2

Feature: Costs little in terms of money, but requires an investment of time.

Benefits: It won't leave you in the lurch and will help you better understand how to interact or motivate others.

Reaction: Are you willing to invest some time and money to learn this skill?

Example 3

Feature: My course is recorded; it is on the Internet.

Advantage: You can take courses anytime and from anywhere, as long as you have an Internet connection.

Reaction: Does that sound like a good idea?

During these steps make sure you are open to the other person's opinions. When people do not see things the way you do, ask them to explain how they see things. Do not put pressure without first understanding why they reject your opinion.

In other words, if during this stage of the persuasion process you detect warning signs in their body language, go back to stage 2 of this process (ask and listen).

Close

This is the last step in reaching a compromise or agreement. After presenting your features, benefits, and getting a reaction, don't be afraid to close the deal.

Learn to ask closing questions such as: Do you agree? So are we going to do it? When do we start? Do we have an agreement? Am I hired? Do you want my help? Are you willing to try?

Note that all these questions are close-ended, "yes" or "no" questions aimed at getting agreement.

Don't be afraid to close more than once. No one likes embarrassment or the unknown, and new things are often embarrassing. That's why people automatically say "no" to anything new or challenging. They may know you are right, but they don't feel ready to take a risk yet.

Statistically, before you get a "yes," you will have to ask for a compromise at least eight times, so you must have enough confidence in yourself and what you are offering. As long as you keep listening respectfully, you won't have to worry.

Let's look at a brief summary of the process of persuasion.

- Build trust by demonstrating integrity, concern and judgment. Make sure you get favorable attention before you speak.
- Ask questions, listen for answers, and confirm your understanding before expressing an opinion.
- Examine the areas of agreement and stop telling people what they already know.
- Show people how they will benefit from your suggestions and ask if they agree with you. Be open to contrary opinions.
- Learn to ask for compromises aimed at closing the process, and don't be afraid to ask for them repeatedly.
- Master every step and you will inevitably be a master of persuasion.

CHAPTER 6:

PRINCIPLES OF PERSUASION

Although every human interaction is different and there is no one way of doing things, psychological studies have discovered some universal principles of persuasion that will help you guide people along your path, and this is just what we will see below.

Empathy

Empathy is an important skill not only in being persuasive, but in any interaction with another person. By learning to put ourselves in another person's shoes, we not only become sensitive to his or her needs and concerns, but also open the door to a healthier and more satisfying life. Learning to actively listen is one of the keys to demonstrating empathy and developing a deeper understanding of the other person and their concerns. It is that deeper understanding that will enable us to be more persuasive.

Active listening consists of listening with undivided attention, looking into the person's eyes and not being distracted by anything. Once the person has finished speaking, you should paraphrase what you heard to show that you were paying attention so that you can later articulate your emotions related to what was just said.

We are all very self-interested, and we have a great tendency to express our opinions when we talk to someone. We need to be aware of this tendency and suppress it. In establishing empathy, it is essential to listen more and talk less, since our goal at this stage is to understand the other party and let them know that they have been heard.

Only when we hear what they have to say and fully understand their position should we give a response, and we must make sure that this response is not too critical. Passing judgment at this stage is a sure way to close off any possibility of offering an alternative and thus persuading.

Credibility

It is all very well to listen to someone to better understand what motivates them, but if after the interaction the other person is still convinced that theirs is the only valid opinion, then you will not have accomplished much. At this point it is important to establish your credibility. Credibility is the feeling of trust and respect that you inspire in others. It can take some time, it doesn't always happen quickly, and at the same time it can be easily lost, so take care of it.

To establish your credibility you have to identify your core values and maintain them. Think about the boundaries you know you can never cross. You also need to be authentic and honest. Honesty is nonnegotiable when it comes to building credibility.

It is important that you understand any topic on which you want to persuade and become an expert in that field. Once you have done this, you should be able to communicate your expertise without sounding arrogant. One way to do this is to include the person you are talking to and ask his or her opinion on the topic, even if you are already aware of the information he or she is presenting.

Communication is part of the process of building your credibility. This is a subject where practice and discipline pay off. At this point you may feel that you are not good at articulating your opinions. Like many other skills, this is an area that you develop as you use it. Focus on expressing yourself clearly and concisely in all your communications. Also, try to remain as impersonal as possible; otherwise, you will weaken your communication. Finally, always try to be transparent. We do not trust people who are very closed and make us believe they are hiding something. Be honest about who you are and what you believe in. Even if people disagree with you, they will maintain a sense of respect for you by being a prepared person who is willing to stand up for yourself.

Similarity

The principle of similarity consists of looking for areas we have in common with others to have a free flow of communication. These areas can be as diverse as liking a sport, having similar goals, or having children of a similar age. Use similarity as a means of breaking down barriers with other people. Research has shown that women are much better at finding similarities than men.

We have to be intentional to find similarities. Think of them as doors to the other person's emotions and trust. One method is to talk about your own passions to see if that triggers any reaction in the other person. However, remember that your goal is not to voice your feelings and opinions, but only to use them as a key to get the other person to communicate with you. Ask important questions and then use your listening skills, remembering that the most interesting people we know are the best listeners.

If talking about your interests does not reveal similarities, then change your strategy. Ask questions. "Where do you live?" "Do you have children?" If at first you don't succeed, don't push too hard and don't turn the conversation into an interrogation. It usually takes at least three meetings before trust is established. If it is a business meeting, make sure you have all the information at hand. Try to find out as much as you can about their goals and use Google and Facebook to do so. You will be surprised at the information you find.

Likability

It is well known that people prefer to accept requests from people they know and like. But this fact can be used even when one is a complete stranger.

What makes one person like another? In general, there are six ways to make people like you:

- The first is to show genuine interest in them. We all need attention, and showing genuine interest in others can make them adopt a positive attitude toward us.
- The second way is to generate joy caused by a smile. A smile is a sign of openness and acceptance of another person.
- The third way is familiarity. It is very effective to pay attention to remembering a person's name and saying it from time to time. Everyone likes to hear their name.
- The fourth way is listening. People like to talk about themselves, so they should be encouraged to do so.
- The fifth way is to speak according to the other person's interests.
- And the sixth way is to make the other person feel important. Sincere and genuine praise often works wonders. It produces an automatic positive reaction.

To explore these points further, I recommend you read Dale Carnegie's book *How to Win Friends and Influence People*, which was published in 1936 and has since established itself as a perennial best seller in the field of self-help.

There is another aspect of the likability principle that has a huge advantage in social interaction: good looks. People spontaneously attribute to physically attractive people a whole range of positive human qualities, such as intelligence, kindness, talents, strength, and self-control. Similarly, we tend to be more supportive of people who look good. Physical appearance influences us without even being aware of the process of our internal reactions.

Authority

Obedience to authority is an established principle of behavior. We are all aware of what human society would be like without organization and authority.

Our attitude toward authority has been formed since childhood, and we continue to react spontaneously to authority in the same way, without sufficient awareness. We assume that a recognized or duly constituted authority has access to information we do not have and for that reason it makes sense to comply with their demands. Submission to such authority becomes automatic, mechanical or blind. Our past experiences have given us sufficient evidence that obedience to a certain authority has served us well, and we have continued to obey without responsible personal reflection.

Some people are born leaders. A true leader has certain qualities that he or she is born with and others that he or she must acquire. Among the qualities acquired are two symbols of authority that are highly valued in today's society: titles and clothing. Titles are relatively difficult to acquire. When a person becomes a specialist in one area of human knowledge, his or her authority is often accepted without further question. This offers a range of possibilities for persuading or influencing those who do not possess their knowledge and skills. But sometimes the mere appearance of possessing such knowledge and skills can cause others to react with the same submission to the person's demands as in a case of actual authority.

The second symbol of authority that can easily make others say "yes" is clothing. Clothing has always been a very important social symbol. Expensive and elegant clothing indicates status, position and intelligence, and thus authority. When people see a person dressed in expensive clothing, this automatically translates into the possession of superior personal qualities. This, along with jewelry and cars, can increase one's power of influence.

"Clothes make the man. Naked people have little or no influence in society."
– Mark Twain

Reciprocity

Reciprocity can be defined as the mutual or cooperative exchange of favors or privileges. In other words, if I do something for you, then you will do something for me. This may seem like a mercenary motivation at first, but it is so prevalent in our society that we often don't even know what happened. Remember the last time you were in a restaurant and you called the waitress for the check? When she arrived, she came with a chocolate; do you think she gave it to you for no reason? Of course she didn't. What she hoped was to stimulate a feeling of gratitude that might make you come back another time, or at least leave a better tip.

It has been shown that when stores give out free samples of a product, they increase sales. This is because by giving something away, the seller has generated a feeling in the buyer that he or she owes him or her: the person who received the item in question is more willing to purchase that product.

What we give does not necessarily have to be something tangible. In a corporate environment, if we compliment a colleague's work, or share credit when congratulating each other on a joint project, we are equally giving something.

Of course, if your donation is perceived as a means to gain some benefit in return, then you will create suspicion and distrust, and your sincerity will be immediately questioned.

Reciprocity is linked to a sense of obligation and that is why it is so exploited. A request that people would surely refuse under normal circumstances can produce a positive response when presented in such a way as to provoke a feeling of indebtedness. Interestingly, such a feeling of indebtedness can also be provoked by an unwanted gift. Even an unwanted favor has the capacity to make us feel indebted.

How can we use the principle of reciprocity? By exploiting the obligation to receive. A person who feels obligated to accept becomes unable to choose to whom he or she owes. As we have said, the sense of obligation due to indebtedness can also be caused by an unsolicited favor. No one likes to be in this state of indebtedness. They feel vehemently the need to get out of that state. Because of this inner discomfort, they are more likely to respond positively to your proposals. There is also another factor that can exert additional pressure: the possibility of social guilt. Accepting favors without returning them is usually socially unacceptable behavior.

Context and time

There are times when a person does not respond positively, even to the most persuasive arguments or techniques. It is always good to assess the moment before embarking on any attempt at persuasion.

Imagine that your wife is feeling very ill and you enter the room wearing the robe she inherited from her grandmother. You want to convince her to undertake a new project, and to cheer her up you congratulate her on her attractive appearance. Bad move. Immediately your credibility will fall to the ground and you will reveal an ulterior motive. Instead, you can try offering her a hot bath and bringing her a cup of tea. You probably won't get what you expected, but at least you won't have raised suspicions to the levels you would have achieved with false compliments. Instead, you will be in a position where you will not have closed doors but rather the opportunity to try another approach at a later time.

Similarly, when you want one of your colleagues to support you in submitting a difficult proposal, it may not be a good idea to try to get his or her support immediately after receiving the news that their salary increase has been rejected. In both examples, it would be best to take a step back and observe. Once you are sure that the other person is receptive to persuasion, that will be the time to make your move.

Interest and need

Interests and needs vary greatly from person to person. What ignites passion in one person may be totally boring to another. In addition, interests and needs are susceptible to great change. Once one need is met, new ones arise.

In order to arouse the interest of others, a proposal must exceed their capabilities to some extent and at the same time it must necessarily be at hand. Something that is too far beyond their capabilities will scare them away. It is best to make people make a small effort to get a benefit, but do not let them become discouraged.

Necessities refer to the most natural aspects of our existence, whether it is mere survival or the development of all our capabilities.

In order to persuade others to do what we want them to do, we must learn to maintain the right balance between evoking, developing and satiating their needs and interests. It is very helpful to awaken people's interest in the different dimensions of their personality (in their thoughts, emotions, desires, sense of values, passions). This will captivate them. And the more we captivate them, the closer we get to our goal.

It is important to work to find out what the other person's needs and interests are and integrate them into your strategic planning. As I mentioned earlier, common interests may not be quite the same, but you can shape reality so that both parties benefit from the persuasion process. There should always be a win-win scenario in any form of persuasion. Otherwise, a sense of manipulation will develop that usually leads to distrust and loss of credibility.

Compromise and consistency

The desire for consistency is one of the main drivers of our behavior. If someone speaks or behaves inconsistently, they are considered unstable or mentally unbalanced. Consistent people, on the other hand, are considered intelligent, strong and stable. Therefore we automatically tend to be consistent, even against our own interests. This principle of mechanical, nonanalytical consistency can be used to persuade others and get an unreasonable mechanical reaction.

How can the tendency to be consistent be used to guide human action? What drives people to maintain their habits so strongly even against their own interests? The answer to this question lies in commitment. If a person is committed, they will make every effort to be consistent with their chosen position. Therefore, to influence them, it is best to make them commit.

If a public commitment is made, the person will feel even more compelled to be consistent. A public commitment puts additional pressure on a person. The same goes for a written commitment. They are more effective than verbal ones.

Rarity

The perceived value of an item, whether a product or a concept, increases as its availability decreases. Such unavailability may be only imaginary, but it has a very real impact. You might try to convince a customer that a gemstone has exceptional value, but if the customer knows that the gemstone can be picked up along the beach, it is very unlikely that you will be able to convince them. However, if you convince them that the stone is very rare and that it is unlikely that they will ever have a chance to buy such a gem again, you suddenly become more persuasive.

Rarity works in two ways. The first has to do with quality. People tend to think that rare things are generally of better quality than things that are easily purchased. They tend to judge quality by availability. The second way rarity operates is related to freedom. When something becomes less available, people feel less free to acquire that something. They will naturally want to defend their freedom, and so their desire to acquire it will increase.

Persistence

Finally, there are times when persistence makes a difference in your persuasion efforts. Persistence is a personality trait that makes someone try despite difficulties and obstacles. When you try something that doesn't seem to work, you always have two options. You can give up, accept that you have failed and sink into depression, or you can try a different approach next time.

In business terms, if you make a presentation to a client and it is rejected on the first try, be polite and keep the doors of communication open for a second chance. Hopefully, you have learned something from your first failure and will be able to correct it when you get a second chance.

"Patience and kindness are power." – Leigh Hunt

CHAPTER 7:
INCREASE YOUR PERSUASIVE POWER

Shaping perception

While reality is objective, our perception of reality is subjective. What does this mean? Although the reality around us is unique, people perceive and interpret it differently. In essence, our perception is a lens through which we interpret reality. If you know how to change that lens, you can change the way people see and interpret reality.

This notion leads to the most common mistake in persuasion. When people need to persuade someone, they usually go straight to the request without considering potentially better psychological strategies that might change how the target perceives their request.

In this section I will teach you how to alter the lens through which people perceive the world around them, and you will learn how to shape their perception so that it is favorable to your situation. Once you alter that lens, any further persuasive tactics will be much more powerful and effective.

"In persuading one must appeal to interest rather than intellect."
– Benjamin Franklin

Your mindset

This may seem like an odd request, but think of a lucky number: Are you thinking of one? Good. Now instinctively and quickly, think of a number between one and ten. Quick! Stop with the first number that comes to mind and don't change your mind.

Do you have the number? Although this method is far from foolproof, you have most likely thought of the number seven.

In this section I will explain the psychological principle behind this phenomenon. In particular, you will learn why imagining a "lucky number" made you think of seven and learn practical techniques for applying this principle in your life.

Perception and behavior

Harvard researchers (Shih, Pittinsky and Ambady, 1999) conducted a study to test the effect of perception. In their study they used people with a strongly stereotyped personality: Asian women. On the one hand, there is a stereotype that identifies Asian women as superior in mathematics, but on the other hand, there is a stereotype that identifies women in general as inferior in mathematics.

The researchers wanted to examine how activating such contrasting patterns might affect their performance on a math test.

Before having the test performed, the researchers asked the two groups of women questions. One group was asked questions related to their gender (regarding makeup, pregnancy, etc.), while the other group was asked questions about their race and heritage (the language they spoke at home, their culture, etc.) Thus, in one group they activated the "woman" pattern, while in the other group they activated the "Asian" pattern.

You can probably guess what happened next when the researchers showed them the math test.

Women who were instructed with their Asian schema performed significantly better than the control group (women who were asked neutral questions), and women who were instructed with their female schema performed significantly worse.

Therefore, any idea associated with a particular pattern (even if we do not believe in that association) can influence our perception and behavior if that pattern is activated.

But how do you activate a schema? The answer is with priming.

Solicitation

Baiting is the means by which a pattern or way of thinking is activated. In the previous study on stereotypes, the "bait" was the questionnaire.

Does this mean that people should be asked to fill out a questionnaire to prepare a pattern?

No, fortunately, there are many easier ways to do this. Research shows that it can be done simply by exposing people to certain words or ideas related to a particular pattern.

But it cannot be lured only with words. It can also be done with images, and this too can happen outside our consciousness. In another study, one group of people was shown the Apple logo, a company with a very creative image, and another group was shown the IBM logo, a company with a very structured and uncreative connotation.

The logos were shown for only thirteen milliseconds, so people were not aware that they were exposed to those logos. However, people who were shown the Apple logo showed more creativity than those exposed to the IBM logo (Fitzsimons, Chartrand, and Fitzsimons, 2008).

How was creativity measured? After luring people with logos, they were asked to name unusual uses for a brick. People who were primed with the Apple logo generated a much longer list than those primed with the IBM logo.

Why does priming work? The answer lies in the propagation of priming.

Propagation of activation

Our brains have a giant interconnected semantic network of knowledge, which contains everything we have learned over time. Each concept in that network, called a node, is connected to other related concepts (the more related they are, the stronger the connection between them). Because of these connections, all other connected nodes are activated whenever one node in the semantic network (through some kind of decoy). This principle is known as activation propagation (Collins and Loftus, 1975).

Remember the lucky number we talked about at the beginning? Activation propagation may explain why thinking about it can make people more likely to choose the number seven.

In essence, the number seven is a node in our semantic network, and it has connections to other nodes. For most people, the number seven node would have connections to things like the seven deadly sins, the seven wonders of the world, and an unimaginable number of other associations. But why would a "lucky number" activate the idea of the number seven? Because that phrase usually combines another idea that is strongly associated with seven: *Snow White and the Seven Dwarfs*.

Because of the connections that exist between these concepts, the propagation of activation is triggered by thoughts converging at the subconscious level to the number seven. If you are forced to choose the first number that appears in your head, you will most likely choose the number seven.

In the next section you will learn how to harness patterns, priming, and activation propagation to improve your ability to persuade.

Cultivating an open mind

So far we have seen how priming a particular schema can trigger the propagation of activation. In this section we will look at the application of a specific schema that you can activate on the people you wish to persuade.

If you want to trigger a more open perception of your goal, simply create a pattern of open-mindedness. It has been found that it is sufficient for the target person to be exposed to words that relate to open-mindedness (e.g., flexible, resilient, moldable, mutable) in order to trigger a more open mind (Hassin, 2008). It has also been shown that it is possible to easily activate schemas by getting people to think about a related concept or by exposing them to examples.

For example, "Remember when you told me I should read Steve Allen's book *How to Identify Lies*? I wasn't interested in it at first, but I read it and loved it."

Making a simple, innocent statement about someone acting openly can also help activate your target's open-mindedness. Just be sure to look for a few examples that fit the context of the situation.

"How do you feel about skydiving? My friend Janet was terrified, but we tried it and loved it."

"My company just hired a new employee, and although I didn't like them at first, I kept an open mind, and we are finally starting to work together very well."

Try to think of a real conversation revolving around the idea of an open mind. The more detailed and elaborate the conversation, the stronger the framework for open-mindedness will be, which will then trigger a more favorable perception of your message.

It is important to remember that you can activate patterns in any order of things and using all the senses. For example, if you want to promote your business in a magazine, make sure your ad appears next to the ad of some other successful business.

It is also possible to use social norms as bait. In one study, a group of students was baited with an image of a library. They were told they were going to visit a library and were prompted with words related to silence and calm. This group of students demonstrated behavior more consistent with the social norm of being in a library than another group that was baited with an image of a train station (Aarts and Dijksterhuis, 2003).

The applications of priming are limited only by your imagination. Whenever you are trying to persuade someone, always think of a possible schema you can activate to leverage the odds in your favor.

The two forms in which we evaluate messages

There are two basic ways to evaluate information presented to us: we use systematic or heuristic processing (Chaiken, 1980).

Systematic processing

When a leader analyzes and studies a report, they use systematic processing; that is, they perform a critical analysis of the information. When we use systematic processing (also known as the central route of persuasion), we are more influenced by the arguments and content of the information.

Heuristic processing

When a leader assesses a report lightly, turning pages quickly, he or she is using heuristic processing, a simple mental evaluation based on quick decision rules. When we use heuristic processing (also known as the peripheral route of persuasion), we are more influenced by simple, irrelevant "peripheral" signals, such as the amount of information available or the aesthetics of the message.

These peripheral signals do not necessarily relate to the strength of a message; however, people often use "heuristics" to make quick judgments about the overall content of information.

Two factors that determine how your message will be evaluated

Two researchers specializing in persuasion, Richard Petty and John Cacioppo (1986), developed a model that describes the factors that determine how a message will be evaluated (systematically or heuristically). The two main factors are motivation and evaluative ability.

Motivation

Your message will be evaluated using systematic processing when the person's motivation is high. When motivation is low, the message will be evaluated using heuristic processing.

This may seem an obvious conclusion, but what exactly determines a person's motivation?

Perhaps the most important aspect is the perceived importance of your message. People will be more motivated to critically evaluate your message when they see that the information is very important to understand.

Capacity

The second factor that determines how your message is evaluated is the person's evaluative capacity. There are two aspects that define a person's evaluative capacity: intellectual capacity and the opportunity to evaluate.

Intellectual capacity: Intellectual capacity is different from general intelligence. If I listen to a talk about perturbation theory in quantum mechanics, I probably have no idea what is being talked about. Does that mean I am stupid? No, it simply means that I don't know enough about this particular topic. In this situation, I will most likely rely on peripheral cues (e.g., the speaker's style, confidence, and presentation) to judge the strength of the content. How else could I evaluate the speech if I do not understand the actual message? In this situation, my intellectual capacity would be too low to use systematic processing to evaluate arguments, so I am forced to rely on peripheral cues.

Timeliness: The second aspect of evaluation ability is related to external constraints. If the person does not have time or many distractions, they will speed up their assessment by relying on peripheral cues, such as the confidence you project and your likability.

Persuasion strategy: Changing the type of evaluation

The previous section explained how people evaluate messages. We have already seen that when people's motivation and abilities are low, they will depend on peripheral cues to judge your message (e.g., number of arguments, aesthetics, and perception of you). When motivation and abilities are high, they will strive to evaluate your message and judge it by the strength of your arguments.

With this knowledge it is possible to:

1. Alter the person's motivation or ability to ensure that your message is positively valued.
2. Predict how the person will evaluate your message so you can tailor it accordingly.

In general, if there are strong reasons why the person should comply with your request, you should make sure that they evaluate those reasons using systematic processing. On the other hand, if you think that the odds are against you because your arguments are too weak, then try to get the person to evaluate your message using heuristic processing, which may cause them to overlook your weak arguments and base judgment on other factors.

How to achieve a systematic process

There are many ways to change people's motivation and their ability to use systematic processing. Two strategies are described in this section: attracting attention and increasing the relevance of your message.

Attracting attention

Most of the time, people are on autopilot and reject new proposals without much thought. You can use the following techniques to get someone's attention.

Offer coffee: Research shows that caffeine significantly increases systematic processing. Researchers exposed students to arguments about voluntary euthanasia in one study, a message they had previously opposed. However, students who consumed a caffeinated beverage were significantly more convinced by the arguments than students who did not consume caffeine (Martin et al., 2007).

Improve message aesthetics: Research shows that improving the aesthetics of your message can also engage people to pay more attention to your arguments (MacInnis, Moorman, and Jaworski, 1991). You've probably been watching TV when a visually striking commercial comes on and grabs your attention. At that moment you think it might contain some important message, so you pay more attention.

Pique technique: Instead of just making an ordinary request, it is possible to present it in a novel way to break the person's autopilot state. To test this claim, a group of researchers dressed up as a beggar and asked for money on the street. They did the experiment three times, first asking for 17 cents (unusual request), a quarter (this is standard US currency, equivalent to 25 cents), and 37 cents (unusual request). What is interesting is that the "beggars" received more money when the request was unusual (17 cents and 37 cents), because people were taken off their autopilot, and forced to evaluate the odd request rather than reject it without consideration (Santos, Leve, and Pratkanis, 1994).

Increasing personal relevance

In addition to attracting the person's attention, a more detailed evaluation of the message can be triggered by increasing perceived usefulness.

A basic technique is to describe the consequences of your message in a particularly vivid way. For example, driver safety commercials are much more effective when they show vivid images of bloody victims, rather than images of test dummies (Rogers and Mewborn, 1976).

You can also tell a story to increase relevance. It is no accident that advertisers on TV try to communicate the benefits of their product through the portrayal of a story or character narrative – why not instead simply describe the benefits of the product? When viewers see a story, they empathize with the characters (especially if they see them as similar), and they begin to imagine themselves using the product in their own lives (Deighton, Romer and McQueen, 1989).

In the next section I will explain how to decrease a person's motivation and abilities so that you can get a simplistic assessment of your message.

How to obtain heuristic processing

If the arguments in your message are rather weak, you will want to rely more on heuristic processing. This is very easy to achieve, as it is the default type of processing for people. In other words, if you don't do anything to increase motivation or ability, people usually perform a simplified evaluation. In any case, there are some techniques to subtly discourage people from abandoning systematic processing.

Increase the complexity of the message

When it comes to persuasion, it is usually said that we should express our message as clearly as possible. Surprisingly, this is not always the best strategy. There are some situations in which increasing the complexity of the message can actually help persuade.

The explanation for this lies in the fluidity of processing. Consider a study involving the description of an online coaching service that helped students get into college. Students perceived that the service was more valuable and were more willing to pay an annual subscription when the coaching service was presented using a light blue font with a white background (a difficult-to-read setting) than when it was presented using a black font with a white background (an easy-to-read setting). Students developed a more favorable evaluation of the coaching service when it was presented in a difficult-to-read format because they mistakenly attributed the difficulty of processing to the higher quality of the service (Thompson and Chandon Ince, 2013).

Presenting the message in a format that is difficult to process can decrease motivation and the ability to evaluate the message itself, which may make people more likely to rely on other factors for their evaluation.

Improving the state of mind

Another factor that may decrease people's motivation to evaluate a message is mood. In general, people who are in a good mood are less likely to critically evaluate a message (Bless et al., 1990).

When we are in a positive mood, we often develop a sense of naive optimism. Unlike positive moods, negative moods lead to greater skepticism. When people are in a negative mood, they subtly assume that there is something wrong with the message, and the uncertainty leads them to analyze that message in more detail.

CHAPTER 8:

TIPS AND TRICKS FOR PERSUADING

What makes people do exactly what YOU want them to do?

People do not buy what you want to sell, but rather what they want to buy. If you want to persuade them, you have to motivate them to act according to their deepest desires. They will then rationally justify their actions. Keep in mind that the main motivating factor in all behavior is the desire to avoid pain, as well as the desire and need for pleasure. These twin forces drive all human behavior. But the truth is that people will always do more to avoid pain than to gain pleasure. Here is a classic example of this principle: Are you more motivated to save a thousand dollars or to prevent someone from stealing a thousand dollars from you? Most people would choose the second option.

Therefore, the way to persuade people is to make them associate your ideas (or your product) in their minds with what they want.

In fact, we tend to associate feelings with situations and objects. If I say the word "Ferrari," what images appear in your mind? What feelings? Maybe you need a means of transportation, but you don't need a Ferrari. You probably want transport in your life, but some people might prefer a subcompact car. Why? Because they associate more pain with the price of a Ferrari than with the pleasure of driving a 500-horsepower car. This point brings us to the following principle: you cannot simply assume people's associations; you must always find people's beliefs and values before persuading them.

The effectiveness of persuasion depends on our ability to assess a situation and choose the right tools. Several psychologists have provided various tips and tricks on this topic, and we will review them in this chapter to help you plan your persuasion strategy.

Sense of urgency

A sense of urgency creates a kind of time scale to increase the need for decision-making. When a decision is left up to people, they will often procrastinate. Creating a timeline instead puts them in the position of needing to focus on that decision. This technique is often used by salespeople when they want to force a sale. Create your deadline. If the person has not made a decision by the deadline, take that option off the table. This may not work in your favor the first time you want to persuade that person, but it will certainly work the rest of the time.

Making the most of fatigue

A tired person is much more vulnerable to being persuaded or manipulated. This is why many military-style interrogations use sleep deprivation. You can use this technique, but be careful not to impose your own agenda on the other person's interests, as it is likely to only result in short-term success.

How to persuade a skeptic

A good way to persuade someone who disagrees with you is to speed up your speech. Imagine someone is talking to you quickly, are you distracted? Can you stop and look for a flaw in his or her argument? Most likely the answer to both questions is no. However, the opposite is also true. When you are talking to someone who is definitely on your side, slow down your speech, let them hear exactly what you are saying, and give them time to agree with you even more.

Speaking with confidence is a great way to increase your power of persuasion. In fact, it has been proven that confidence is undoubtedly even better than accuracy when it comes to persuading others. Most people prefer to receive advice and learn from someone who shows confidence and self-assurance, even going so far as to forgive and forget a history of mistakes. To persuade successfully, you need to be able to communicate your confidence.

An oath can persuade

Just a light oath, of course. If you throw out your words with profanity, you will lose all the credibility and respect you could have gained. Recently, a group of researchers gathered eighty-eight participants and divided them into three groups. Each group had to listen to one of three slightly different speeches. The only real difference was that one of the speeches included a short oath at the beginning of the speech. The second speech had the oath at the end, and the third did not include an oath.

When the researchers measured the attitudes of each group of participants, they found that they were more influenced by the speech that included the oath at the beginning. The audience paid more attention, which led to greater persuasion. It should be noted that none of the three groups changed the way they perceived the speaker's credibility; it simply changed the effect of the speech, showing that a small oath can do wonders for your power of persuasion.

Ask them to agree with you on something

If you want to get someone to do what you want, start by giving them something they can actually agree to. In one of their studies, Robert Wyre and Jing Xu discovered the effect generated by prior agreement. In one of the tests, a group of students listened to a speech by John McCain (Republican), while in the other test they listened to a speech by Barack Obama (Democrat); after both speeches they watched a Toyota commercial.

Republican students were more easily swayed by the Toyota advertisement after seeing John McCain, while Democrats were convinced after seeing Barack Obama.

When you are trying to sell something, whether it is a service, a product, or an idea, provide a statement or opinion that your audience can certainly agree with from the beginning, even if it has nothing to do with the idea you are selling.

A balanced argument is more convincing

If what you say or sell is likely to elicit criticism, you should never hide the weakness or flaws in your arguments. We all fear that drawing attention to a flaw or weakness might undermine our position, but in fact it is the opposite.

Over the years, psychologists have compared unilateral arguments with bilateral arguments to see which were more persuasive in different contexts. Daniel O'Keefe of the University of Illinois has compiled the results of 107 studies on persuasion conducted over the past fifty years, involving 20,111 people (O'Keefe, 1999, *Communication Yearbook*).

The results of this analysis showed that across different types of persuasive messages and with varied audiences, bilateral arguments were more persuasive than their unilateral equivalents.

Generally speaking, people are not stupid. Knowing how to persuade them means recognizing that they can think. If you avoid mentioning the negative side of the argument, your audience will know it and be less likely to believe what you say. If necessary, point out the disadvantages or shortcomings of your product or proposal.

Seeing is believing

People will definitely believe you more if they can see the evidence for themselves. Research by Eric Johnson, Ye Li and Lisa Zaval examined global warming and its relationship to local climate at the time. Study participants in Australia and the United States were asked to rate how much they believe in global warming. They were also asked to rate whether the temperature on that day was colder, warmer or normal for the time of year. It was found that when people believed it was warmer, they believed in global warming more than when they said it was colder than normal.

In another related study, the same questions were asked, but at the same time participants were asked to make a donation to a nonprofit organization working to combat global warming. When the day was perceived as warmer, the study participants donated more than four times the amount they donated when the day was perceived as colder than normal.

Therefore, if you want to get people to follow you and believe in your message, you have to do it in the right situation to support your claims. You need to use storytelling, emotions, and mental imagery to build the perfect scenario for the story you want to sell.

Keep in mind that, strictly speaking, you don't need to use real situations; just learn how to draw pictures in people's minds. A very powerful word to add to your arsenal is "imagine." Imagine that you have the tools to convince anyone; can you feel the power that would give you?

The strange paradox of choice

The more you have to offer, the less likely people are to make a decision. The following is a study conducted at two tasting stands set up in a supermarket. One stand offered only six flavors of jam, while the other offered twenty-four flavors. The tasters received a coupon to purchase jam.

The booth that offered more jam options attracted many more customers, but most of them only tasted, and very few bought. The booth that offered a limited number of flavors significantly increased sales. In the booth with twenty-four choices, only 3 percent of those who tasted used their voucher, while in the booth with six choices this percentage rose to 30 percent.

The message is that if you have a lot of products or ideas, it is good to spend some time filtering to offer a limited range and increase your chances of persuasion.

Repetition is key

Repetition of words or language patterns makes you not only remember them, but accept what you hear as true. Our brains are excellent pattern seekers, and this is a very useful skill. Repetition creates a pattern, which (naturally) attracts our attention.

Repetition creates familiarity. When we are in a supermarket, we are much more likely to buy familiar brands, even if we have never tried that particular product before.

Think about the last time you bought a pair of shoes – did you pick them out and then try them on several times before you bought them? If so, you are like most people. People have to repeat things several times before they are convinced. Three times is a popular number for this.

Repeat the key benefits or main parts of your message several times. Effective advertising campaigns do exactly that. Research shows that even in a group, if one person repeats their opinion often enough, they will be considered representative of the entire group.

Men respond better to emails than to face-to-face meetings

Research conducted in 2002 showed that men seem to be much more receptive to email than to an in-person discussion. This is because by using email, men avoid their tendency to be competitive. In contrast, women respond better to in-person discussions because they tend to be more relationship oriented.

Research suggests that while email can be a way to reach more men by circumventing their competitive nature, this is only true if the relationship is distant. If a man is in a close relationship, talking face-to-face works best. If you want to convince a man to do something, and you don't know him very well, try email first.

Limit the amount of information

In 2007, Carnegie Mellon University conducted a study on the effect of history versus data. The researchers were George Lowenstein, Deborah Small, and Paul Slovic. The subjects were asked to donate to a really bad situation that was happening in Africa. The information that was provided was filled with statistics about food shortages in Malawi and severe drought in Zambia.

In a second version of the experiment, a donation was requested for a specific person, a starving child in Zambia named Rokia. Her picture was shown and people were invited to donate in her aid.

On average, those who participated in the first experiment (the data-based experiment) donated $1.14 while those who participated in the story-based experiment donated an average of $2.38.

A third experiment was then carried out. Participants were told about Rokia, but also about drought and food shortage statistics. In this case, participants donated an average of $1.43.

The lesson to be learned is that too much data is overwhelming. In a problem seemingly so big, most people think their contribution will make no difference and donate only a small amount of money.

If you are going to sell to men, use photos of women

A study of the consumer credit market found that showing pictures of women was as effective as lowering the interest rate. A credit company sent out letters proposing short-term loans at a randomly generated interest rate. Those letters also contained some psychological characteristics, which were also randomized. As expected, the interest rate had a significant impact on whether or not the loan was taken out. What was surprising was that some of the random psychological characteristics also had an effect.

The loan company said, "For male customers, including a photo of a woman in the letter significantly increased loan acceptance. The effect was similar to lowering the interest rate by 4.5 percentage points. No statistically significant patterns were found for female customers. Overall, these results suggest a very powerful effect on male customers when they see a female photo. However, the performance characteristics of this study do not allow us to isolate a specific mechanism for this effect. It may be due to the positive impact of a female photo or the negative impact of a male photo."

The next time you target a male-only audience, use a female image and you will notice a significant increase in conversions.

Convince only those who can be convinced

We can all be persuaded at one time or another, as long as the timing and context are right. However, some people may require great powers of persuasion. Take a look at politicians and their campaigns. They focus their money and time almost exclusively on the small groups of voters who are responsible for determining the outcome of an election. The first step to successful persuasion is to identify and focus on the people who can, at that point, be persuaded to adopt your point of view.

Disinterested people cannot be persuaded

You simply cannot persuade someone who is not really interested in what you have to say. In general, the human race is primarily concerned with its individual being and spends most of its time thinking about three things: health, love and money. The first step in convincing someone is to learn how to talk to that person about themselves. Appeal to their self-interest and you will get their attention. Keep doing that and you will keep their attention long enough to persuade them.

Reciprocity is a weapon

We have already examined the principle of reciprocity in a previous section. Like it or not, most of the time, when someone does something for you, you feel an innate obligation to return the favor. It is the way we are wired, a survival instinct that goes back millions of years. You can use this reciprocity to your advantage by giving someone something they want, then you can ask for something much more valuable, and they will feel an obligation to comply. The principle of reciprocity is much more effective if you are the first giver and if your gift is personal and unexpected.

Find out their expectations and exceed them

One of the keys to persuasion is learning to manage the expectations of others. If a CEO promises their employees a 20 percent pay raise and then gives them 30 percent, they will have more persuasive power over their employees than a CEO who promises 20 percent and gives only 10 percent. Learn to understand what others expect from you and then give them more.

Make it look rare

Nowadays almost everything has value on a relative scale. Often we want something because someone else has it or because it is hard to get. If you want to persuade people, it may not be enough to point out the benefits of the ideas or services you are offering. It can be much more effective to talk about their uniqueness and what your subject might be missing out on. This will create a sense of rarity, so the less there is, the more people will want.

Be flexible in your behavior

Have you thought about why children are often much more persuasive than adults? It is simply because they are willing to enact a wide repertoire of behaviors to get what they want: crying, being charming, begging, trying to negotiate, and so on. The more varied behaviors you have in your repertoire, the more persuasive you are likely to be.

Folk charm

Popularity is an interesting thing. It feeds on itself. A Japanese ice cream chain successfully launched its product in New York through a clever marketing strategy. They paid dozens of people to stand in line and buy their ice cream. When passersby saw all those people, they didn't even ask what product was on sale – they simply joined the line so they could "get theirs."

McDonald's proudly announces "over one billion sales," making it clearly a "popular choice." In brief,

Popular for others = Good for me

Exclusivity

Have you ever walked into one of those high-end stores that have only two or three products displayed in a huge space? Exclusivity is the correct name. In today's globalized world, exclusivity is particularly attractive. That is why it is very common to see messages such as "limited edition," "limited production," or "limited number available." This is a powerful illusion, and you have to be smart enough to frame and present your best ideas in the context of exclusivity.

For example, "The information you will learn in this book is not available to the average reader" or "I only accept twenty-four new students each year to participate in my successful course in persuasion with language models."

The concept of exclusivity is very concrete. No interpretation is needed; there is no need to find out what it means. "Only ten available" means exactly that. It is easy to choose.

Superiority by association

Car buyers choose Mercedes Benz and BMW because in their minds these high-end cars are immediately identified as "superior." The luxury car owner believes that the qualities of the car (such as value, exclusivity, uniqueness, and superiority) reflect their own characteristics.

Superiority is also the reason why perfumes such as Chanel and Gucci are so popular. Although the perfume is definitely "just a perfume," its designer's name lends an air of "haute couture" along with its fragrance.

However, superiority does not automatically come at a high price. An idea/product/service is superior when it is truly better than the rest. What you offer can be superior in terms of quality, capacity, comfort, availability, speed, value for money, and so on.

All you have to do is emphasize what is superior in your proposal and make it clear that those who take advantage of your words will be perceived as superior by those who were not so clever.

Show and explain

I recently went to buy a book lamp. While I was looking at the products, the salesman came in with batteries in his hand. He asked me which model I was considering, put the batteries in it, and showed me all the available light intensities and positions. I was impressed, not by the lamp (which was pretty standard), but by the effectiveness of this persuasive strategy. By showing me how his product worked, the salesman made his profit-making ideas completely tangible.

The first thing you must do is decide how to visually demonstrate the benefits of your ideas. You need to convey the feelings of satisfaction, confidence, happiness, superiority, security, and so on that your proposal provides.

Tearing down walls

There are two walls hiding behind people's fears and objections. It doesn't matter if you're selling an idea or a car. Your mission is to walk through it, over it, under it, or alongside it.

Wall 1: How can I be sure I am doing the right thing?

Your strategy should be to provide useful educational information. Provide factual information in an unbiased way that allows the other person to make an informed decision. It is sufficient to present bare facts. Sharing knowledge is a powerful way to break down walls of resistance. When people feel that you are informing them, they will respect you and appreciate your openness and honesty.

Wall 2: Are you a person to be trusted?

Your strategy should be to provide some kind of social proof. Use the old "such and such says" technique. Research facts, figures and third-party quotes. When an authoritative person supports your ideas, you will benefit from a phenomenon known as reflected integrity.

Preemptive strike

This is a great way to keep the other person's objections at bay. It consists of responding to any objections before the person raises them. This strategy serves two purposes. First, it responds to the person's doubts, and second, you use it as a new opportunity to talk about the advantages and benefits you have to offer.

Questions are a powerful resource. If a person asks you questions, it means he or she is interested in what you are saying. Even if an objection sounds like a resounding "no," it's not a no at all – it's just a request for a solution to a problem.

Using fear

Fear is a basic human instinct and is one of the easiest "emotional buttons" to push. Although the pursuit of pleasure seems to drive most people's decisions, it is actually their desire to avoid pain that makes the difference.

Fear is a negative emotion that a person wants to alleviate as quickly as possible. This makes it a valuable weapon in your arsenal of persuasion. Show people a fear-creating prospect, then show them how they can eliminate it and you will generate an immediate response. In the next section we will talk more about the persuasive power of fear.

CHAPTER 9:

PERSUASION FORMULAS AND HOW TO USE THEM

"I prefer to try to persuade a man, because once I persuade him, he will stay with me. If I frighten him, he will stay with me as long as he is afraid, and then he will leave." – Dwight D. Eisenhower

Persuasion is an art that can be combined with science to formulate effective techniques. The key is to use proven methodologies to achieve the exact results desired. Many experts have spent years formulating techniques that work for them. By adhering to their formulas you will be able to replicate persuasive results with relative consistency.

These formulas are parallel tools to the step-by-step persuasion procedure we saw in one of the previous chapters, so you should use them to improve your skills and not as a substitute for the initial procedure.

That said, there is no one generic formula that works for everyone. As a novice persuader, you will have to experiment until you determine which formulas work for certain people. Most of the formulas we will look at below were generally developed by marketing and advertising experts, but they are applicable to any aspect of life.

AIDA

This formula is a classic when it comes to selling and persuading, and it has proven to be very effective. AIDA stands for attention, interest, desire and action.

These four ideas are the basis. When you use this method, you begin to attract the audience's attention. You should start with an attractive main title, that is, make a great first impression. Your appearance, the way you dress, your body language, your walk, your eye contact, your vocal tone, your status. All of these things are essential for a first impression. You will capture others' interest by telling them things that will come up in conversation and show how much you understand their wants. Then you move on to desire. This is where you put the idea of what you want and explain how it fits perfectly with your audience's interest. Finally, you'll wrap it up by adding the action they need to take to fulfill their desire. And voila, your message has a clear and systematic means of reaching your audience and encouraging them to take action on what you want.

Car ads use AIDA in a cheeky way. An ad might begin with an attractive woman or perhaps with enlarging the car. Then the unique features of that car are showcased, while a voice explains why we should buy it and how it will improve our lives. Most ads end the same way: leaving viewers wanting to visit their dealership.

PAS

This formula is an effective alternative to AIDA. It works a little differently, focusing on problem-solving. This method is shorter and more direct. PAS stands for problem-action-solution. You start by mentioning a problem. It must be a problem that your audience needs to address. Then you stir up emotions by exaggerating the problem. Explain how the issue is negatively affecting their lives. Be specific and highlight as many negative aspects as possible. The key is to increase the intensity of the situation.

Using this method, you will connect with your audience, play on their fears, and then show them a solution that will give you what you want. For greater effectiveness you can use an anecdote or make things personal. For this formula to work, it is important to understand your audience's concerns. Also, empower your solutions by filling them with positive keywords to help increase the impact of your message.

FAB

This method shows how fabulous your arguments are. Apple has perfected the art of FAB in its advertisements. In fact, most product descriptions use this strategy by focusing on all the fabulous benefits awaiting their users. The technique is most effective when talking about new ideas or alternative ideas that do not necessarily solve a big objective problem.

FAB tactics focus on explaining features, advantages, and benefits. You will begin by listing some interesting features of your product, along with the service or desired outcome it provides. It is important that you highlight the *how* of your product's benefits to your audience before revealing all of its positive aspects. This will increase your credibility. The benefits of these features are listed below. You should talk about the specific benefits and the immediate benefits achievable. Finally, close by focusing on the major long-term benefits. In this technique it is crucial to mention the positive aspects and not the negative aspects. Explain how your fabulous solution enriches life in the short and long term.

IPPP

This method is used by some people unconsciously, and it is very effective because people are very receptive to this technique. The acronym IPPP stands for image, promise, proof and pressure. As is the case with FAB, it focuses on the positive aspects, but instead of listing the characteristics, you draw a picture with words and focus on attracting attention by promising to solve their problem. Next, as a means of building trust, you will have to support your ideas with sources or demonstrations. Then, you must find a way to prove your point. This is a crucial step in gaining credibility. Ultimately, you will deliver the coup de grace with a call to action.

Research your sources and choose those that are most convincing to you. Also, remember that your promises and evidence should also be in alignment.

Star – history – solution

Are you a good storyteller? This technique may be right for you. It is simple, effective and convincing. With this method, while generating confidence in your topic, you also keep your audience's interest constant.

First, create a scene with a main character, your star, the protagonist of your story. It could be yourself, a product, your audience, or even a made-up character. Then get people's attention with your story. Create tension and explain a problem. Define the problem your star has to overcome. Then, as in any great story, your star must find a solution to their problem.

You can use this method to create a hypothetical situation for your audience to consider, or an anecdote to gain some confidence. Through the use of a third-person perspective to frame your proposals, you can present your ideas and solutions objectively.

Five basic objections

It is very easy to think of excuses, and this technique is based on just that. There are five statements that condition any change: I don't have enough time, I don't have enough money, I don't need it, I don't believe you, and it won't work for me.

In this method, you take one or more of these excuses and start countering them with the proposed solution. The more problems you address, the better your argument will be.

Forest method

This method is a comprehensive technique that combines different aspects of persuasion. It uses alliteration, facts, opinion, repetition, examples and statistics. You can use each element of your reasons in any order you wish to form a wonderfully effective persuasion trick. This works great in speeches or long conversations.

Probably, subconsciously you have already used some of the methods we have reviewed. Some may be more effective than others depending on your strengths, so until you find your style, you should continue to train in your new skills.

CHAPTER 10:

LANGUAGE MODELS

One of the first things we need to learn to persuade effectively is something commonly known as "the guard at the door." You have probably already heard of the conscious mind and the subconscious mind. The guard at the door essentially works with the subconscious mind: Its mission is to evaluate the information that comes in and determine if it is true before it gets it through the door. We need this guard; otherwise, we would accept all the information we receive.

The challenge for every communicator, for every influential person, is to overcome this guard, but how do you do it? This is exactly what we will look at in the following sections.

How to overcome the "guard at the door"

The easiest way to get past the guard at the door is to present information in such a way that it is overlooked by the guard, and for this we will make use of language patterns. To explain this process we will use the brainwave model, which is a very simplified model of a very complex topic, but as you will notice it is sufficient to start using this material.

Beta state

In this state, the brain produces predominantly beta waves. This is the normal state of when you are awake, and is characterized by being alert and active, for example, when you are very busy with some task. In this state you are task oriented. The important thing to understand here is that when you are in the beta state, it is very difficult for new information to enter the brain unfiltered. The guard is at the door. This does not mean that someone cannot be persuaded in the beta state, but it is much more difficult.

Alpha state

In this state the brain produces predominantly alpha waves. This state is also known as "the gateway to the subconscious mind." It is characterized by a more relaxed and peaceful state of mind. You are usually in an alpha state when you are deeply absorbed in a television program or a book.

Let us think about the differences with the beta state. When someone is in a predominantly alpha state, they are more absorbed in their thoughts and feelings than in the beta state. It is commonly said that the person is in a trance, and I am not referring to the trance state shown in movies or hypnotic shows, but to a more receptive state of mind. The key is that when someone is in the alpha state, the guard at the door is more inactive and new information is more likely to enter. In the alpha state the person becomes more open to suggestion.

When people watch TV for a long period of time they enter an alpha state, which advertisers obviously exploit. This does not mean that the person becomes a zombie, only that he or she becomes more suggestible.

You need to understand that we naturally move in and out of alpha and beta states during the day, but we can also intentionally generate them. Here are some language models for using this knowledge.

Language patterns to overcome the guard at the door

By using the following words and phrases in your conversations you will be much more convincing because of the way the brain processes information and language at the subconscious level. These patterns allow you to inject ideas into people's subconscious with minimal resistance.

"Could you ..."

The essence is that you are not saying "you have to ..." You're just saying that you want someone to imagine how relaxing and enjoyable a massage might be. You can be direct and just say, "Imagine how relaxing a massage would be now," and that might work, but by adding "might" at the beginning, you're telling the guard to relax, because it's an indirect thing. You're saying, "OK, everything I'm going to say next is just hypothetical; it's not necessarily true." Any indirect phrase tends to relax the guard. However, you should not abuse this phrase and always speak indirectly, because you will make people angry.

"You shouldn't ..."

This is a model of negation. Interestingly, the subconscious mind does not process negations in the same way as the conscious mind. So when there is a negation, the guard at the door of the mind becomes inactive and the message can pass freely, and at the same time the subconscious mind does not understand negations and processes only the affirmative part of the sentence.

For example, "You should not buy this book now without considering its benefits." What the subconscious understands is that "you should buy this book now without considering its benefits."

Another example, "You should not feel good about buying this car without thinking about it."

"It is not necessary ..."

This is another pattern of denial. You don't have to understand how these patterns work internally to make them work for you; all you have to do is use them and make them part of your vocabulary.

"It is not necessary to feel completely comfortable using these phrases now, as they will come naturally with practice." In this case we put two phrases together to increase the persuasive power of the message.

One of the advantages of using these phrases is that they force you to shape your ideas in terms of what you want, rather than what you don't want. For example, if you want someone to be quieter, don't say "don't talk so loud," but formulate your sentences with words related to what you want, such as "quiet," "shush," or "quieter."

"If ..."

This sentence creates less resistance because it is an indirect sentence that begins with the word "if," and allows the person to experience the behavior or condition you are describing. For example, "If you were completely convinced that this was an excellent opportunity, how would you feel?"

Another example, "If you bought this computer, would you put it on your desk or somewhere else?"

"When ..."

This is one of my favorites. It is very simple and very effective. This sentence contains the assumption that the person will act to experience the conditions that follow. For example, "When you realize how powerful these sentences are, you will look for every opportunity to put them into practice."

Another example, "When you feel completely comfortable, I would like to know what you think."

"You don't have to ..."

This is another pattern of denial. By not giving the instruction to do something, no resistance is created. For example, "You don't have to believe what you read; you can take action and convince yourself that it is true based on your experience."

Another example, "You must not make the decision now, at least until you feel you have complete confidence that it is the right thing to do." What the conscious mind understands is "you must not ...," so the guard at the door becomes inactive, but what is really registered in the subconscious mind is "make the decision now," "you feel you have complete confidence" and "it is the right thing to do."

"What would it be like if ..."

This sentence immediately tells the guard at the door to relax, since it contains the words "would" and "if," so it is something hypothetical. What makes this sentence so powerful is that it inherently includes the instruction "imagine."

Examples:

"What would it be like if we joined forces and did business together?"

"What would it be like if you woke up tomorrow and started living the life you really want to live?"

"What would it be like if you drove this new car and showed it to your wife?"

"As if ..."

This sentence is a great connector of ideas. For example, "What would it be like if you were so persuasive, as if people seemed to be in a trance while you were speaking?" If you model your sentences in accordance with people's desires, they will always be inclined to listen to you.

"Like when ..."

This phrase is very effective because it forces the person to remember the emotions, conditions, feelings, and thoughts related to what you are talking about. You do not have to strive to create a fictitious emotional state, but it will suffice to use an emotional state that that person has already experienced. For example, "When you finish reading this book, you will feel as you did when you were a child and received that Christmas present you were waiting for."

For more persuasion techniques with language models, I recommend you read my book *Persuasion and Influence with Language Models*.

CHAPTER 11:

THE ART OF PERSUASIVE WRITING

Until now, we have examined methods of persuasion that are particularly effective during face-to-face interactions. However, we are not always in front of the person we want to persuade. In fact, much of our communication today takes place online. According to email service providers, two billion emails are sent every day, not counting messages through social networks and other online communication methods. Therefore, learning the art of persuasive writing is increasingly important.

As with direct communication, the key is practice and conscious intent. Take the following techniques and make them a mandatory checklist for every time you need to write an email.

It starts with a catchy title

Buzzfeed is a news site that makes millions of dollars using this tactic – you can use it in your daily life. Catchy headlines attract readers by using words specifically designed to grab their attention and make them want to read more. This is exactly what you need to do. Suppose you want to send out an email newsletter promoting your latest antiaging product. You can write in the subject line, "Check this out," or something more appealing to the reader, such as, "I'll show you how to get youthful skin in a week."

Start with the positive

Explain to readers why they should continue reading your message. List each benefit briefly and concisely to help them see the benefits of what you offer. This will keep their attention and encourage them to continue reading with a more positive attitude. Now it is time to present all the benefits of your proposal.

Anticipate readers' questions

To establish your credibility and trust, make sure your email contains all the information readers may need to clarify any questions they may have. Actively evaluate possible questions before you write your message. This will help readers identify them and give you the credibility and momentum you need to make your persuasion work effectively.

Turn your words into a story

Most human beings like to hear a good story. Make sure your stories connect with your audience. Advertising agencies have long used this strategy by selling products through short stories in their television commercials. The more interesting your story, the more effective your message will be.

Use keywords

Just like the title of your email, its message should be easy to understand and contain keywords. Words such as "earn," "new," "free," "rich," and "you" are able to discreetly attract a person's attention. Find the right keywords for your audience.

Do not repeat

Reinforcing what you have said is important, but don't do it too often in written communication. Keep your points as short and simple as possible. The more words you use, the more attention you lose.

Design your email

Don't just write paragraph after paragraph. Visually appealing texts are very important when it comes to persuading readers. Add paragraphs, bullets or numbered points, pictures and headings if possible. Don't be afraid to use some color and bold words.

Using these elements in all your email communications will maximize your effectiveness in the persuasion game. Just be sure to practice as much as possible.

CHAPTER 12:
EXTRA TECHNIQUES OF PERSUASION

"The future influences both the present and the past."
– Friedrich Nietzsche

Persuasion trick: Conveying high expectations

On January 12, 2007, a violinist played for forty-five minutes at the Enfant Plaza Metro station in Washington, DC. During those forty-five minutes some people stopped to donate a couple of dollars, but nothing unusual happened. Almost everyone walked at their usual pace without stopping to listen or pay attention. What was so surprising about this? The violinist was Joshua Bell, one of the world's greatest violinists. Two days after his performance at the subway station, Bell performed in a crowded Boston theater, with an average ticket price of $100 per seat.

This surprising phenomenon relates to our expectations and how they shape our perception of the world. Our expectations largely dictate our perception of the world. Whenever we develop expectations for a certain event, our brain shapes our perception of that event according to our expectations.

We see what we expect to see. We hear what we expect to hear. We feel what we expect to feel.

The placebo effect is a clear example of this concept. When researchers test a new drug, one group of patients is given the real drug and other people are given a fake version of the drug (i.e., a placebo) that has no effect. This procedure is necessary because our expectations can also dictate the outcome of treatments.

Although the placebo effect is typically associated with drug trials, expectations affect all aspects of our lives.

Recent research has revealed interesting findings about whether people prefer Coke or Pepsi. Because Coke is the dominant brand, most people have developed an expectation that Coke tastes better. When people know what they are drinking, most prefer Coke; however, when taste tests are blind (when people do not know which one they are drinking), the expectation is eliminated and most people prefer the taste of Pepsi (McClure et al., 2004).

Expectations can not only shape our perception but can also influence our behavior. In another experiment, some people bought an energy drink at a normal price of $1.89, while others bought the same energy drink at a discounted price of $0.89. The researchers wanted to examine whether knowledge of the price of the drink could influence performance on a mental task. The results were quite enlightening. People who bought the drink at the regular price performed much better than those who bought it at a discount, even though the drink was exactly the same (Shiv, Carmon, and Ariely, 2005). People who bought the drink at a regular price developed higher expectations about the effectiveness of the drink, resulting in better performance on the mental task, while people who bought it at a discounted price developed lower expectations, resulting in worse performance on the mental task. Even something as simple as the price of an energy drink can convey certain expectations, which can influence our perception and behavior.

If you want people to perceive something more favorably, you have to convey high expectations, as these expectations will become a goal that will form their perception.

Foot-in-the-door technique

This powerful persuasion technique was popularized by Robert Cialdini (2001). When you need to persuade people to meet a large request, you can increase your chances of success by making a smaller request first.

Since you are more likely to get a result with a smaller request, that initial result will cause the person to develop a more open attitude when you make the second request.

One study has already examined this principle (Freedman and Fraser, 1966). Under the guise of road workers, two researchers tried to influence households to comply with a rather large request: the installation of a large, ugly sign saying "Drive Carefully" on the facades of houses. When they made the request on their own, the researchers were only able to get 17 percent of people to agree. Weeks later they repeated the experiment with other households, but first they made a small request: to install a small three-inch sign that said "Be a safe driver." Almost all the families agreed to install this small sign. Within a few weeks, the researchers went back to the same families and asked them to install the large sign: they were 76 percent successful this time.

Lowball procedure

In addition to using a small query to guarantee you a result with a second, larger query, you can do the same thing and increase the same query's size.

This technique is known as the lowball procedure and is a common tactic used by salespeople to influence their customers (Cialdini, 2001). In fact, you may have already been a victim of this tactic by a salesperson at a car dealership, where it is frequently used.

Imagine going to a dealership and having just negotiated a great discount with the salesperson. As the salesperson walks into the office to draw up the paperwork, you stay and enjoy the vehicle, happy that you got a deal. However, the reality is that the seller will probably stay in their office and let time pass so that you can fantasize about your vehicle. After a few minutes, the seller returns with the sad news: The manager has not approved the sale, and the fantastic "deal" has been discounted by only $500. However, by that time the salesperson has already triggered your momentum by getting an initial result, and as a result, you will have the right inertia to adapt to the new situation. You have already fantasized about your new car, and you have demonstrated a behavior that suggested you wanted the car. Like a puppet master pulling the strings of a puppet, you have just given control of your strings to the salesperson, who will pull them toward acceptance of the new request made.

CHAPTER 13:

BASIC CONCEPTS OF NEUROLINGUISTIC PROGRAMMING

"Don't wait. It will never be the appropriate time. Start wherever you are, by whatever means available to you. Better means you will find along the way."
– Napoleon Hill

We will begin this adventure of perfecting our persuasion and influence skills by shedding some light on the winding path of neurolinguistic programming, also known as the science of success. Neurolinguistic programming, or NLP, deals with the influence language has on our mental programming and the rest of the functions of our nervous system. Read it again, "NLP deals with the influence of language on our mental programming and the rest of our nervous system functions." This means that the functioning of our nervous (neuro) system is closely related to our language (linguistic) capacity and the strategies (programming) through which we behave and relate. Expressed in simpler terms, NLP is a powerful tool for manipulating our conscious and unconscious mental processes, and also for manipulating other people's mental processes.

Consequently, with language, we can create or change perceptions in ourselves or others. Every day we interact and communicate with other people through language, our actions, our body language and also through our facial expressions, and this interaction has a huge influence on how we feel, how we react to certain situations and the effect we will have on other people. It is worth clarifying that this is not a complete course in NLP, but a practical course on how to use language to persuade and influence, so in this chapter we will focus on learning the fundamentals of neurolinguistic programming to understand how our brains work and, consequently, understand how the persuasion techniques and speech patterns that we will see in later chapters operate.

Are you ready? Then let's get started.

NLP is defined as the study of human excellence, and demonstrates how to communicate effectively and influence others. It was developed in the 1970s by a group of professionals who studied successful people with the goal of analyzing human behavior. Richard Bandler (psychologist), John Grinder (linguist) and Gregory Bateson (anthropologist) were part of the group. They considered language styles, brain patterns and how words and actions come together to create certain mental programming or sequences of behavior.

Since then, NLP has continued to develop, giving us a greater understanding of the processes of thoughts, speech patterns, and human behavior, providing us with patterns that help us process human experiences and understand the way people think, feel, and react.

Controlling your communication with the outside world will determine your degree of success with others in personal, emotional, social and economic spheres. However, here NLP allows us to make a fundamental distinction. The degree of success you perceive inwardly is a result of how you communicate with yourself. What I mean is that what you perceive is not the result of what really happens in life, but only the interpretation you give to it. In other words, you will feel and behave according to how you have decided to perceive your experiences. Now let me ask you: What if you had the tools to manipulate the way people perceive your messages? Think about that for a moment.

Obviously, you would be able to elicit the emotions and actions you desire, and that is precisely what you will learn in this book.

Below, we will get down to the facts and explore the basic principles of NLP that we will need to learn powerful persuasion techniques. We will discuss rapport, representational systems, beliefs, conditioning, metaprograms and metamodels. We will also see three patterns or redefinition techniques for changing the focus of others and your own.

CHAPTER 14:

RAPPORT

Effective communication in relationships is based on mutual respect between people and is often carried out intuitively. You must demonstrate genuine interest by observing how the other person reacts to what you say and identifying the key words or phrases that produce a reaction. Rapport is related not only to what you say, but also to your actions and body language, which you are not normally aware of.

To build rapport, you need to be aware of how people communicate and how they use their gestures, body posture, tone of voice, words, and so on. One of the basic aspects of building rapport is the "concordance and reflex" technique created by Milton Erickson in the early 1970s during his clinical hypnotherapy work. With this technique you try to imitate the body language of the person you are speaking with. This is something that is clearly seen in recent couples who unconsciously imitate each other's body positions.

You can try the following exercise with another person to experience the powerful effect of concordance and reflex. You can do this with your partner or a friend, but at first do not alert them to what you are doing. Do this: While the person is talking about something they really enjoyed, such as a party or a hobby, listen carefully and imitate their gestures and postures. After a minute, change your behavior and do the opposite; that is, make gestures that do not coincide with those of the other person while he or she continues talking. Wait a few minutes and go back to imitating their gestures.

This exercise consists of reflecting, doing the opposite and reflecting again. After the exercise, explain to the other person what you did so that they can comment on what they observed and what they felt. Normally, it should have been very difficult for the other person to keep talking while you were behaving in the opposite way to his or her body language. This is the power of relationship. It can open or close minds and hearts. However, be careful when applying it. If you overdo it, it will look like you are making fun of the other person, and you will get the opposite effect to the one you desire.

We will now discuss another fundamental concept of NLP: representational systems.

CHAPTER 15:

REPRESENTATIONAL SYSTEMS OR SENSES

You probably already know that there are five main senses (sight, hearing, touch, taste and smell) and that we use our senses to interpret the world around us. However, although most people share these five senses, we "interpret" information differently. For example, imagine a garden. Take a few moments to think about the details.

Did you?

What did you think about?

Of all the people who are reading these lines, some will think of the smell of grass, while others will think of the color of flowers, and still others will think of birdsong. Thus, the same scene may mean different things to different people, depending on one's preferred sense.

What do we need to know all this for?

The importance of this information lies in the fact that you increase rapport and improve communication when you talk to someone by adapting your words to that person's preferred meaning. Can you follow along? As you will see throughout the book, as we go along, each concept will intertwine with the previous one, so that by the time you have read the last page you will have completed the big puzzle of communicating using speech patterns. It is important that you trust that the content of this book was designed with this goal in mind, and so if at any point you feel lost, have full confidence that eventually the pieces will come together and everything will make sense.

So let's move on. We were left at the point that if you choose your words carefully to fit the preferred senses of the person listening, you will increase your chances of being persuasive. But now you may be asking yourself, "How can I know a person's preferred sense?"

This is a very good question. Now, although we know we have five main senses, it is very common for people to have one dominant sense, the most common being sight, hearing or touch, and the best way to find out is by paying attention to people's language and characteristics. Let's look at three very common cases.

Predominantly visual people

As the name implies, these are people who interpret the world primarily through the sense of sight. It is common for them to be very orderly people in their personal lives and at work, they are very conscious of their appearance, and they can seem hyperkinetic as they are always busy doing something. When speaking and thinking, they tend to move their eyes upward and express themselves using terms that relate to the sense of sight, for example:

"I see what you are referring to."

"I grasped the image."

"He looks good."

"I can imagine."

"Let's have a look."

"Keep an eye on it."

Predominantly auditory people

These are people who have a quieter and more serene behavior than those who are visually oriented. When speaking and thinking, they tend to move their eyes to the side, that is, toward their ears, and they tend to express themselves using terms that relate to the sense of hearing, for example:

"I heard what you said."

"Sounds good."

"Listen."

"It sounds familiar."

"I tuned into this idea."

"He is on a different frequency."

Predominantly kinesthetic people

Kinesthetically oriented people are particularly relaxed and quiet . They prefer wearing comfortable clothes rather than being fashionable. The men do not wear ties, and women even avoid makeup. They prefer the pleasures of life, food and perfume. When talking and thinking, they tend to move their eyes downward and to the right. They tend to express themselves using terms that refer to the sense of touch, taste and smell, for example:

"It looks good."

"It is easy to handle."

"This touched me."

"Grapple with reality."

"He has a weak character."

"Lend a hand."

"It makes my hair stand up."

These descriptions may seem like overgeneralizations, but if you concentrate on carefully observing the people you talk to, you will be surprised at how accurate they are. The senses can be sharpened even more. For example, if we ask two people to visualize a beach, they will surely imagine two very different scenes, based on their mental maps. Probably one of the people will see a colorful, people-filled, sunny beach of which they are a part, as if they were watching a movie, while the other person will imagine a black-and-white, stationary beach of which they are not a part.

These kinds of more subtle distinctions are called sub-modalities, and their beauty lies in the fact that you can refine or change sub-modalities to change feelings and emotions when it comes to positive or negative situations. Read this again because it is very important: "You can refine or change sub-modalities to change feelings and emotions."

For example, changing an image in your mind from colors to black and white will make it less vivid, until you can completely disassociate from the emotions. Or maybe you can add some humor to a stressful situation, perhaps by imagining the other person as a cartoon character. The possibilities are endless, and you can make these changes either in the moment or later when you remember the situation. So the way you feel about something changes instantly when the sub-modes in your mind change.

I know that if this is your first encounter with NLP, it may seem hard to believe, and that's because we don't come into this world with an instruction manual telling us how to use our brains, but now you are learning to. We will soon be implementing exercises that will allow you to experience the power of these techniques.

Now let's recap what we have just learned: By knowing your own sub-modalities, you will be able to know how to get out of a limiting state of mind and into one that is full of energy and transmits power. However, this is not limited to what you can do in your own mind, as you can produce the same effect in other people if you discover their preferred senses.

Let's look at a list with the main sub-modes. Keep the list for reference, as we will use it later in an exercise to control your mind.

Visual sub-modes:

- Color
- Gloss
- Contrast
- Static or moving
- Blurred or in focus
- Near or far
- Small or large

Auditory sub-modes:

- Volume
- Tone
- Duration
- Location
- Stereo or mono
- Words and sounds
- Rhythm

Kinesthetic sub-modes:

- Temperature
- Location
- Intensity
- Consistency

- Weight
- Pressure
- Measure

It is important to remember that everyone interprets situations through his or her own perceptions, thus creating his or her own reality; consequently, experiences are individual and each person will have their own unique interpretation of events, depending on how he or she experiences through the senses (sight, hearing, taste, touch and smell) and how he or she internally interprets information.

Does it sound complicated? Don't worry. I wrote this book with the goal of helping you, and you don't need to memorize all this. Later, in the speech patterns section, I will teach you an amazing technique for tapping into people's representational systems and effectively persuading them without even looking at them. With that pattern, all you'll have to do is say a single word.

To be persuasive, we need to understand how people make decisions, and we also need to know what their main representational system is so that we can express our message so that it fits the style of their mind's functioning. For example, when you have to talk to a visually oriented person, you won't need to speak slowly and breathe deeply, since doing so will only succeed in making them lose patience and get on their nerves. Therefore, below, we will elaborate further on how to identify the sub-modes and mental strategies of others.

CHAPTER 16:
CONDITIONING

A conditioning is a stimulus that reminds you of certain events and can change your state positively or negatively. So it is something very powerful, because it allows us to instantly access states of great strength, or great weakness, although it is hard to want the latter, don't you think?

These stimuli can include all the senses (sight, hearing, touch, taste and smell) and can be internal and external. It could be a simple word, a sentence, a touch, a smell or an object.

We all use conditionings, constantly, and, in fact, it is impossible to stop doing so. Each type of conditioning is an association that is made between thought, ideas, feelings or states and a given stimulus. Recall Pavlov's experiments. We learned Ivan Pavlov let some hungry dogs sniff meat, and they began to produce a considerable amount of saliva, sensing that powerful stimulus, and when they were in that state of intense salivation, Pavlov rang a bell. After a short time, meat was no longer needed to produce salivation; the dogs only needed the sound of the bell and began to produce saliva, as if they had smelled meat. In this way, Pavlov created a neurological link in his dogs between the sound of the bell, the sensation of hunger and the salivation reflex.

We live in a world full of stimulus-response situations, so much of human behavior consists of unconsciously programmed responses; for example, under tension, some people automatically smoke, drink or even take drugs. The key to what you are reading right now is to become aware of this process, so that if existing conditioning within yourself or within others is not helpful, it can be eliminated and replaced by new stimulus-response constraints. Can you think of any situation where you would like to create reflexes in people to produce a determined response based on a stimulus you created? Very well – below you will learn how conditioning is created.

If a person is in a very intense state and, if under these conditions, he or she is simultaneously given a certain stimulus that coincides with the climax of that stimulus, a neurological constraint will be created between it and the stimulus, in the same way as Pavlov's dogs. In this way, whenever that stimulus is used in the future, the same intense state will be generated automatically.

In most of us, random conditioning has been formed over time. We are bombarded by the messages that come from television, radio and daily life. Some turn into conditionings and some do not, and it usually happens by accident. However, we are here to learn how to create conditionings consciously. The process of creating conditioning in yourself, or in others, consists of two simple steps. First, you must bring yourself, or the other person, into exactly the state you wish to condition. At this point, you must create the specific and exclusive stimulus several times, just as the subject is in the climax of the said state.

Another way to create conditioning in another person is to ask them to recall an experience in which they were in the state you wish to elicit. The goal of this point is for the person to experience the same sensations, just as if they were reliving the experience. When this happens, you will be able to observe changes in his or her physiology (facial expressions, posture, breathing), and as soon as you realize that the climax is approaching, you should quickly administer the specific, well-differentiated stimulus several times, for example, gentle pressure on that person's left arm. Obviously, these are not covert persuasion strategies, since in this particular chapter we are just learning about how conditioning works, so the proposed exercises must be done with the other person's consent.

For conditioning to be effective, the person must be in a fully associated and coincident state throughout his or her body at the time the stimulus is administered. If you do it when the person is thinking about something else, the stimulus will dissipate or be associated with different signals. In addition, the stimulus must be administered at the climax of the experience. If you are late or too early, it will lose intensity. To know what this state is, you can observe the person, or ask them directly to tell you when they feel the same sensation as the original experience. Also consider that the stimulus must send a different and unmistakable signal to the brain; for example, a handshake would not be suitable, since it is too common a gesture. In conclusion, in order for conditioning to work, it must be reproduced exactly, several times.

This is a process that takes practice, and in the same way as for the exercises we have seen so far, the best way to master it is to practice on yourself. Remember that when it comes to learning to control the processes of the mind, you are your own laboratory, so now we are going to do a little experiment to produce conditioning on you.

For this exercise you need to select three states or sensations that you would like to have available to you when it is convenient for you. Condition them to a specific part of your body so that you can easily access them. Let's say you want to have the ability to make decisions quickly and confidently, and let's also say that to condition this feeling, you decide to use the knuckle of the index finger of your right hand.

Now think of an occasion in your life when you felt fully resolved and secure. Mentally immerse yourself in that situation and associate yourself completely with it. Relive the experience and, at its climax, when you feel fully decided and confident, press your knuckle and mentally say to yourself, "I can!" Now think of another similar experience and, when you are at the peak of this process, repeat the same pressure and the same phrase. Do this six or seven times to accumulate a powerful set of conditionings. Then, think of a decision you have to make, consider all the factors you need to know in order to make it, and throw the conditioning signal.

It really is that simple, although it requires practice. Mastering the NLP concepts and skills we have seen so far produces incredible synergy, as they enhance each other. I trust that you have now practiced these techniques, and I hope you will continue to use them. Now, armed with this knowledge, you can send powerful signals to your own or another person's mind to make things turn in your favor. In the third part of the book we will look at a technique for "changing or weakening beliefs" that uses these principles and will enable you to become a more effective communicator.

We now know that what you say and how you say it affects others, and can influence and persuade in different ways. But to use these skills, you need to listen very carefully to what is being said so that you notice the words and phrases used by others. Below, to continue with the basic concepts of neurolinguistic programming, we will discuss two very important concepts: metaprograms and metamodels.

CHAPTER 17:

CIALDINI'S PRINCIPLES OF PERSUASION

Arguably, Robert Cialdini is one of the world's leading experts on what influence and persuasion are all about. After decades of research and study, Cialdini identified the basic areas of influence, and below we will look at these five principles and how they can be used to influence others.

Principle 1: Reciprocity

Humans have evolved to be social creatures and, as a result, people tend to return favors. If someone says or gives something helpful to another person, that person usually feels an instinctive need to "repay" this favor. A perfect example of the use of the reciprocity principle is the Hare Krishna movement. They give you a flower (or in some cases a book) and tell you that it is a gift. However, as soon as the "gift" is accepted, the disciple asks for a donation. This technique has greatly increased the donations they receive.

There are, virtually, endless ways to use the principle of reciprocity in your favor, but remember this:

Normally, when we do someone a favor, we miss the opportunity to take advantage of this principle. When they thank us, we are used to saying, "Don't worry about it" or "Don't worry, it's nothing." By doing so, you are unintentionally belittling the favor you did. You have put across the idea that it really is no big deal, and so what will those around you feel? They will feel that they don't owe you anything. From now on, say, "I know you would have done the same for me." No more, no less. This is a friendly response, but it still leaves the feeling of doubt and the space to be reciprocated. Make sure you use the power of reciprocity to your benefit and don't take away importance from the favors you have done for others.

Principle 2: Commitment and consistency

Committing to a goal or idea, whether in written or oral form, makes it significantly more likely that a person will keep the commitment, even if he or she has no incentive to do so, or if the initial motivation or incentive fades after making the agreement. The reason behind this principle is that commitment makes us want to be consistent with the image we have of ourselves.

A study conducted in the mid-1960s by psychologists Jonathan Freedman and Scott Fraser demonstrated this fact by asking some homeowners to mount a large, ugly billboard on their homes that said "DRIVE PRUDENTLY." Of course, it was an absurd and quite outlandish request, so only 17 percent of homeowners agreed to that crazy request when the researchers went door to door posing as volunteers.

However, all it took was a small, seemingly insignificant adjustment in their application, and the researchers were able to get that percentage as high as 76 percent.

How did they manage to get such an incredibly different answer?

Here's the solution: Two weeks earlier, the researchers had asked the owners to display a small three-inch sign that said "BE A PRUDENT DRIVER." Since this request was minimal, virtually everyone agreed. However, when another "volunteer" returned a couple of weeks later, those owners were much more receptive to the second request for a larger sign.

Why did agreeing to put up a business card-sized sign lead to property owners being willing to sacrifice their yard for a billboard the size of a poster?

Human beings have a natural tendency to be consistent in all areas of their lives. Once someone commits to something, makes a decision, performs an action or takes a position, they strive to make sure that all future behaviors are consistent with that first behavior. This principle of commitment and consistency explains why the foot-in-the-door technique is so effective (we will look at this technique in the third part of the book).

Consequently, to use the principle of compromise and consistency in your favor, you have to get someone to do something small to establish a minimum compromise with his or her self-image, at which point he or she will be more likely to keep that commitment and accept greater demands consistent with that self-image.

Principle 3: Social proof

Imagine you are driving in a city where you have never been. You are hungry. There are two restaurants. One has a full parking lot, and the line of customers comes up outside the restaurant. The other restaurant is practically empty. There is hardly anyone there.

Which one do you go to?

In nine out of ten cases, people choose the full one. They will not go there "despite" it being full, but "because" it is full. The assumption is that if everyone else is there, it means it is probably a better restaurant than the other.

This is social proof in action.

Social proof is the reason we see so many advertising campaigns with slogans like "Join 300,000 other satisfied members" or "Used by millions of satisfied customers," or even "As seen on TV."

Social proof is one of the most powerful methods of persuasion. Harness it by showing testimonials, opinions, people using your product, the number of products sold, and so on. You can also use social proof in smaller situations, such as creating consensus; for example, if most people agree with something, then those who are less sure will be more likely to agree with that consensus.

Principle 4: Authority

People tend to obey authority figures, even if what they are asked to do is questionable or, as some studies have revealed, downright unethical.

A famous example of the power that apparent authority has over people is the Milgram experiment.

During the Milgram experiment, some authoritarian-looking researchers ordered the participants to inflict strong and painful electric shocks on some actors (even though the participants did not know that the people they were theoretically giving the shock to were only actors), who screamed and begged for them to stop. However, given the overwhelming power of authority, virtually all participants continued to obey orders and give the shocks to their victims, who were screaming.

Another example of the power of authority comes from a TV reporter who placed a sign on an ATM machine that read "OUT OF SERVICE. HAND OVER DEPOSITS TO THE POLICE." Looking authoritative and wearing a police uniform, a badge on his chest and a baton on his belt, the reporter managed to get $10,000 in cash and checks in just two hours. In addition to this, he also managed to get credit cards, social security numbers, account numbers, PIN codes and other private information from people. Surprisingly (or perhaps just as to be imagined), only one person objected and questioned the apparent authority of the police. When the reporter showed his true identity and revealed the deception, asking the victims why they had so easily surrendered their money and private information, they all answered pretty much the same thing: "For the uniform."

Does that sound like overkill?

Authority is not just about strength or perceived authority, such as that of a policeman. It is also about appearance. Imagine you are considering taking a course to become a successful entrepreneur. You have two options: seminar A or seminar B.

Seminar A is taught by an entrepreneur who drives a Ferrari, dresses in fancy custom-made clothes, wears a watch that seems to be worth as much as your annual salary, and generally looks like a very successful entrepreneur.

Seminar B is taught by an impresario who drives a beat-up 1998 Toyota, is overweight, apparently has not washed his hair in several days, and if it were not for his old, low-quality suit, would look more like a butcher in the middle of his workday than a successful entrepreneur.

Which seminar would you choose? Nine out of ten people would go to seminar A, because in this particular case, the person giving the seminar seems much more credible than the neglected guy in seminar B. However, the reality is that the guy in seminar A might be a con man, even if we judge him by his appearance as someone who has a good knowledge of the subject and we are persuaded.

So, suppose you are not likely to want to dress up as a policeman, complete with sign and baton. In that case, you can use the power of authority to your benefit by displaying confident body language and speaking in a firm, assured-sounding, authoritative voice.

Principle 5: Pleasure

People are more likely to be influenced or persuaded by people they like.

At one point in my life, I provided consulting to a company of door-to-door salespeople and noticed an interesting trend. The salespeople who made the most sales (and earned the most from commissions) were not the ones who talked to the most people. In fact, there was an almost negative correlation between the number of prospects and the number of sales.

This is because the salespeople who were closing most sales were spending more time with each potential customer. They were developing a "relationship." They talked to them, got to know them, and as a result, they ended up being liked by them, so they had a better chance of persuading them. This is the power of liking.

Some time ago I read an article in Forbes, "Intelligence is overrated: what it really takes to succeed," that referred to the research of Nobel Prize-winning psychologist Daniel Kahneman. What Kahneman's research found was that people prefer to do business with someone they like and trust (as opposed to the other way around). This, of course, is by no means a surprise, but here's what's interesting: people prefer to do business with those they like even if those people offer a lower quality product or service and at a higher price.

Many of the principles we have seen seem to go against logic, but human beings do not make decisions based on logic. The point of knowing these principles of influence is that they allow us to take advantage of the three basic human needs that move us all, and these three needs, or motivating factors, are the key to understanding how to influence or persuade people (from Cialdini and Goldstein, 2004). These necessities are the explanation of why language patterns work, which we will see in the third part of the book. But what are these three needs that drive all of us? We will look at them below.

Need for affiliation

For the most part, human beings are social beings, so we want to feel accepted. Rejection is not a pleasant thing, and we would do anything to avoid it. We answer people who ask us a question, because by doing so we send them a message about our sociability. We try to please others by behaving in a way that we think is attractive, such as agreeing with them or complimenting them. We seek approval from specific people, but not only that, we also seek approval from society at large. We want what we do, think and believe to be in line with what others do, think and believe. It is not impossible to be different, but it is a difficult thing.

The pleasure and reciprocity techniques mentioned earlier clearly appeal to our desire for affiliation, as do many other techniques of persuasion and influence, and the people who are best at influencing others take advantage of this need and give us something to follow.

Need for precision

People who don't care about doing things correctly get nowhere in life. To achieve our goals in a complex world, we have to constantly look for the best way to act. It could be precision in social situations, such as how to deal with the boss or how to make friends, or it could also be precision in financial matters, such as how to administer a business. Whatever the contention, people always strive for the "right" answer.

People who have influence are able to identify our need to do things correctly and therefore try to offer us something that appeals to our need for precision. For example, experts or authority figures have great influence on people because they offer a vision or a "right" way of doing things, especially those that do not involve too much thinking. The social proof technique appeals to our desire to be precise because we assume that other people are likely to be right and we do not want to show disagreement.

Need to maintain a positive and consistent self-concept

People want to protect their vision of themselves because it takes a lot of time and effort to build a semi-coherent vision of ourselves and our place in the world. We work hard to maintain our self-esteem, we want to continue to believe what we believe, and we want to fulfill the commitments we have made in the past. In an inconsistent world, we should at least be consistent with ourselves.

Persuaders and influential people can exploit this need by appealing to our sense of self-consistency. A trivial but instructive example is the foot-in-the-door technique, which we will see in part three of the book. In that case, people capable of influence ask to accept a small request before making a larger one. Since people somehow feel that it would be contradictory to accept one request and then reject another, they will tend to say yes again. As you will see later, people go to surprising lengths in order to maintain a positive view of themselves.

We all want to be accurate, be accepted by others, and maintain a good concept of ourselves, although we are rarely aware of these needs. The speech patterns you will learn later aim to meet one or more of these needs, and with this in mind, you can tailor your persuasive intents to the particular characteristics of your listener, rather than relying on generic techniques. Whether you are at work and have to deal with your boss, or at home arguing with a neighbor, you can benefit by thinking about the unconscious motivating factors of others, and in this way decide how to construct your message, according to his or her needs.

Now that we know the principles of influence and the basic needs that each person wants to satisfy, you may be wondering: How can we structure our message?

This is a very good question. Fortunately, there are specific rules and patterns that will allow us to elaborate and enhance our persuasive messages. In the next chapter we will see what these rules are, and remember that even if you don't learn any language patterns yet, already these rules alone are very effective persuasion techniques. These rules are the mortar that will allow you to combine language patterns to build powerful, persuasive messages.

CHAPTER 18:

OVERCOMING PEOPLE'S PSYCHOLOGICAL RESISTANCE

You could now persuade your partner, children, boss, employees, customers, and so on, but there is only one problem: No one wants to be influenced or persuaded. We all feel an overwhelming urge to exercise free will in our choices and actions, so we use a variety of psychological resistance techniques to defend ourselves against the powers of persuasion. And we are well trained. We resist thousands of advertising messages every day, and if you didn't know how to say no, you'd be broke in a few days.

In an interesting study by Matthew T. Crawford, Allen R. McConnell, AR Lewis and Steven J. Sherman, participants were presented with two similar football teams, and they had to bet on one of them. When another participant (who was actually one of the researchers) said, "You definitely have to pick team X," the participants picked the opposite team 76.5 percent of the time. This is the power of reverse psychology in action.

In their book *Resistance and Persuasion*, Eric Knowles and Jay Linn identify four psychological barriers to persuasion and, as a result, the word "if" can help magically break each of them. To explain the four barriers of resistance, let's look at them with an example.

Let's say someone is trying to sell you a life insurance policy. Technically, this insurance policy is the best thing for you, but the four barriers of resistance threaten to keep you from making a good decision.

In this example, the salesperson knows that this life insurance is perfect for you; however, they do not know that you are a difficult customer. The salesperson says, "Have you ever considered taking out a life insurance policy? I think policy X is perfect for you."

Well, in this case the salesperson used what is known as "direct selling," and when this happens, the first resistance appears inside you and so you respond, "Don't try to sell me life insurance that I don't need!"

You feel under pressure. You realize they want to sell you something and you raise your defenses to escape the situation. This is called "reactance" and it is a key barrier. You feel that you are being pressured, so you start to retreat, and once you get into this mode of thinking, no matter what the salesperson says, they will not be able to convince you. End game.

If the seller had tried to use the word "if" to create a hypothetical, non-threatening situation, things might have been very different. This is what they might have said:

"If a person in the same circumstance as you had come to me, I would have recommended policy X."

It looks harmless, doesn't it?

The salesperson is not recommending anything to you directly. They are talking about another imaginary person. The word "if" breaks through the resistance because, otherwise, the barrier of "reactance" would have rejected any kind of approach. Unfortunately for you, your resistance continues not to allow you to see the great opportunity before you, and here comes the next barrier of resistance: "mistrust." Here's what you respond to:

"They only say that because they would earn a very high commission on it! Sellers are all the same; they just want to cheat people."

This is certainly understandable. There are some sellers who have hidden motives, but although I do not know the exact number, I also know that they are not all scammers. There is a possibility that this particular consultant just wants to be helpful.

The distrust barrier tends to appear in absolute terms, and the phrase "All salespeople just want to cheat people" is a perfect example of this kind of generalization. Fortunately, the word "if" moves people away from the dangerous territory of absolutes and brings them back to a more realistic point of view. It is in this way that the honest salesperson might use some "what ifs" to help you overcome your distrust:

"He's right, there are salesmen who are always trying to cheat. I have seen it myself. But, if there were a cure for cancer, to explain it to people we would still have to 'sell' them the idea. Does this by any chance mean that we are cheating? Of course it doesn't. So, let's be honest, policy X is not a cure for cancer, but what if it was the cure for your life insurance problem?"

This skillful move by our salesperson has helped you get past the mistrust stage, but you are still not done fighting.

"Maybe, but I'm not convinced about the price." (Or any other possible objection.)

Here the third barrier of resistance appears: "control." This is when, during the decision-making process, you weigh all the pros and cons a little more thoroughly and carefully. By discussing the details of policy X with an honest salesperson, its strengths are highlighted, but its weaknesses also come to light. It is these weaknesses that can create this psychological barrier. There is a legitimate possibility that control will ruin this negotiation and not allow you to take advantage of this opportunity. Fortunately, our honest salesperson again has the word "if" at their disposal.

"If I could show you a way to get the full benefits of policy X at an extremely affordable price, would you do it?"

This particular course of action is so effective that even dishonest salespeople are successful when they use it. If you accept it, then you will have worked hard enough. If, on the other hand, you say "not now," you will only be disagreeing with yourself. Once again, this is a sentence to which it is easier to say yes, because it is only hypothetical and the weight of reality continues to be absent.

At this point, three barriers have already been overcome. For our honest salesperson, it is a simple matter of stating the facts and allowing the customer to make the best decision. However, despite the fact that at this point we are both in pretty good agreement about policy X, there is still a barrier of resistance to overcome. If our honest salesperson does not help you overcome this barrier to get you a better insurance policy with a higher price, they will have failed and you will be forced to settle for the second best offer.

This is the resistance barrier that Knowles and Linn call "inertia." The hardest thing for a human being is not climbing Mount Everest. It is not raising a child. It is not creating a work of art. Psychologists say the hardest thing for a human being is to change his or her behavior patterns. We detest change. Inertia is the difference between saying we are going to do something and actually doing it. In this case, you may be convinced that you'd better take out that insurance policy; you say you're going to do it – but not now. You need a few days to think about it, and eventually you won't take out that new affordable policy because you don't like change.

Again, our honest salesperson will save you from procrastination and build a bridge over the abyss of inertia using the word "if." Here's how:

"Many things can happen in a week. What would happen to your family if, God forbid, something happened to you in these days?" How would you feel about your decision to postpone this action?

Now you are experiencing what psychologists call "anticipation and remorse." In the study by Crawford, McConnell, Lewis and Sherman that we mentioned earlier, they talk about a condition of anticipated remorse. So if the researcher, instead of just saying, "You definitely have to pick team

X," had added phrases like, "Why would you regret it if you didn't pick them and they won" or "How bad would you feel if you didn't pick them, and they ended up winning?"

Remorse anticipation had a decisive effect on a participant's decision. Before, 76.5 percent of participants had NOT chosen the recommended team, but with the anticipation of remorse, participants completely changed their behavior and chose the recommended team 73 percent of the time. It seems that their resistance vanished almost completely: the skillful use of the word "if" tends to produce this effect.

Now let's look at other "if" applications.

How to use the power of "if" with complainers

You know the kind. They are the ones for whom nothing is ever good enough. Everything is miserable and they feel it is their duty to inform others of how bad things are. It is very common to be surrounded by negativity in the workplace, and it is time to use the word "if" to put an end to it.

These are the five steps to deal with people who complain chronically:

Step 1: Check all the negativity and determine what the complainer's main concerns are. Don't be ashamed to get out a notebook and start making a list of their problems as they complain, just "to make sure everything is done right."

Step 2: Repeat the list of complaints out loud to confirm that they are right.

Step 3: Quickly convey them to an optimist and ask them for suggestions to solve the situation instead of other problems.

Step 4: Provide a plan of action.

Step 5: Close the issue. People who complain don't know how to end a conversation, and, in fact, they won't notice all those social signals they are used to getting when they complain. You need to interrupt them. Be firm and clear, if necessary.

In theory, this all sounds very good, but at some point in step 3 (when you ask for a solution), those who chronically complain will say, "I don't know how to solve it. That's why I'm coming to you." This is where you need to use the power of "what if." Try doing this:

"If you had a magic wand and could make anything happen, in the world, what would your life be like without this problem?"

Normally people fail to focus on solutions because they get trapped in the how. You can't figure out "how" to improve a condition until you really know what its solution is. You have to help them focus on the "what," and to do that you have to use the word "if."

The phrase, "If I had a magic wand," sends the message, "For now forget the 'how' and let's simply think about 'what' we want."

Why is it so important to make them imagine a positive outcome? Because the moment they imagine and explain it, it is more likely to actually happen. This might sound silly or too simplistic, but never underestimate the ability of the human mind to influence outcomes. Research conducted by SJ Sherman, RB Skov, EF Hervitz and CB Stock at Indiana University found that when people describe a hypothetical outcome in a positive way, they not only increase their chance of success, but also improve their actual efforts. So, the key lies in the hypothetical element, and the word "if" takes them right there.

Now let's look at a variation of the schema to use the hypothetical element.

Use of the hypothetical element

One of the most common reasons I hear from people who say they cannot present their ideas is that they are afraid of rejection. That is why we will now look at a set of words that you can use to present something to almost any person, at any time, and without having to worry about rejection at all. The pattern is as follows:

"I'm not sure you'd be interested in that, but ..."

Let us take a moment to understand how this simple structure works.

By beginning the sentence with "I'm not sure you'd be interested in that, but ...," you are making sure that the listener's unconscious mind is listening to you, and at the same time you are telling them, "I'm not pressuring you at all." By suggesting that the listener may not be interested, you obviously increase their curiosity, and it is this increase in curiosity that attracts them. This command affects an internal control that says you have to make a decision, and the gentle approach ensures that this decision gives the impression of being not pressured but free. However, the real magic happens with the word at the end of this sentence, a word that, ironically, should normally be avoided in all conversations: the word "but."

We'll look at the use of this word in detail later, but for now imagine you get a comment from your boss that starts by saying, "You know you're a really good team member; you've done a really good job, but you need to improve some things." What is the one part you will remember? As we will see later, the word "but" negates everything that was said before it, so when you say to someone, "I'm not sure you might be interested in this, but ...," the little voice inside the listener's mind says, "You may want to find out."

Let's look at some examples:

"I'm not sure you'd be interested, but would you like to know how (insert results and benefits of your product or service)?"

"I'm not sure you'd be interested, but we have plans for Saturday, and if you'd like you can join us."

"I'm not sure if you would be interested, but this option is only available for this month, and I would hate for you to lose out."

This rejection-free approach leads to a simple result, and one of two things will happen: the person listening to you will ask for more information because they are really interested or, in the worst case, they will say they will think about it.

CHAPTER 19:

CHANGING PEOPLE'S EMOTIONAL STATE

Why would you want to change a person's emotional state? All beliefs, decisions and thoughts have emotional content. Sometimes this emotional content is large, but other times it is so small that we don't even know it is there. Somehow, emotional content is always present in everything we do, and it plays a major role in our decisions. Have you noticed how your beliefs about yourself and the world change depending on the state of mind you are in? All the decisions you made while you were happy, sad or bored would have been different if you were in a different state of mind. So if we can change the emotion, then we can change the belief, thought or idea.

Can you now understand the importance of learning how to change people's emotional state? Below, you will learn how to do so. Keep in mind that we will start with the basics and gradually add more elements until we reach a complete strategy.

We have to remember that when you talk to other people, they create an internal representation of what you are saying, and they have to do that for the sentence to make sense. If I say, "Don't get excited by this idea," you have to make an internal representation of the emotion in order for the sentence to make sense.

Now, if I wanted, I could make you experience a few more sensations. For example, I could construct a sentence like, "When I really have a good idea, I start to feel a tingle in my stomach that starts to rise up to my chest as I keep thinking about all the things I could do with that new concept. That's how I know it's really a good idea ..."

In this case something subtle and very interesting happened. You will notice that in the example above I gave you instructions on how you should feel when you have a good idea. You will also notice that I started by talking about me and ended by talking about you. People rarely realize this, although many people use this way naturally and without realizing it in their conversations. In NLP jargon, this is known as referential index change, and it is a perfect way to start a conversation by talking about yourself and concluding by talking about others, without them noticing.

Now let's add one more element to sharpen our technique, and see the importance of questions.

If I say, "I want you to be intrigued now," you will have to form an internal representation to understand what I am saying, although you will have nothing with which to connect these elements, since this sentence will not have much effect on you, will it? Now, if I say, "When I am intrigued I feel a kind of buzzing in my head and I feel an attraction to the topic, as if it were a magnet from which your mind cannot escape until it has learned more," I am giving you instructions on how to be intrigued, and I am using a change in the referential index. In this case, we are probably a little closer than in the first example, but you are still not connecting the elements.

But what if instead of the previous sentence, you just ask yourself, "How do you know when you feel immense curiosity?" In this case you will have to look within yourself to find the answers and discover your own curiosity process, so the associated emotions and feelings will be more meaningful to you.

If I were now to say, "When I am intrigued I feel a kind of buzzing in my head and a strong attraction to the subject, as if it were a magnet from which your mind cannot turn away until it has learned more. How do you know when you feel immense curiosity?" In this case your brain will want to give an answer to this question, and to do so it will have to try both sentences and compare the results, so with my words I have made sure that you access your feelings.

Before we continue, let's do a little summary of what you've learned so that you keep your mind clear. Now you know the following four ways to access a person's emotions, from the weakest to the strongest:

1. Directly provide internal representations. "You might find it interesting."
2. Provide a process for emotions. "When I am interested in a topic it is because suddenly I see all the possibilities, and I can easily imagine all the new ways of applying this knowledge."
3. Asking questions. "How do you know when you are really interested in a topic?"
4. Use a combination of the previous three. "I don't know if you will find this topic interesting. Certainly, when I first discovered these new concepts, I immediately started thinking of a flood of possible applications, and the interest turned into excitement as you go along imagining all the applications. I felt an increase in the temperature inside my chest as I came up with new ideas all the time. How do you know when your interest turns into excitement?"

Very well, now that we know how to access people's emotions, let's look at a language pattern that will allow you to get people emotionally involved in what you are saying.

We know that people make decisions through emotions and use reason and logic to justify those decisions. Fortunately, an NLP schema takes advantage of this condition to evoke the emotional state you want and assumes that the person listening will do what you say. It is very simple to use. The schema is as follows:

"Think how much <positive emotion> you will feel when you finally <what you want me to do, think or feel>"

Let's look at some examples:

"Think of the happiness you will feel when you finally have a beautiful garden."

"Think of how much relief you will feel when you finally leave our practice." (Maybe a dentist's.)

"Think how peaceful your family will be when they finally move into this house."

You need to think about the kind of emotions you would like the person to feel and how that person could achieve the results he or she wants by doing what you want. In this sense, the word "finally" is especially useful when the outcome may be difficult (such as losing weight or quitting smoking), and the person has already tried various solutions before meeting you.

This is a very versatile pattern, and you can modify it by adding a positive emotion and a third person or group. For example:

"Think of the envy of your neighbors when they see you driving such a car."

The central idea of this schema is this: If you tell people why they want or need to do something, you will only get the reputation of being desperate. However, show them how your ideas and skills can bring them money, protection, comfort, security, pride, love, or whatever they want. Those same people will begin to value your perspective more, and when people give weight to your perspective, you have become a persuasive person.

Consequently, to be persuasive you must be able to provoke emotional states for fun and for money. Richard Bandler said, "It doesn't matter what you think you are selling. It is simply about feelings and emotions." Remember that people buy feelings and emotions and then justify their decision with logic and reason, so if you want to take advantage of this aspect of human nature, you have to discover the feelings they want and give them in the form of benefits.

What kind of benefits? Below is a list of benefits that people normally seek (in no particular order):

- Making money
- Saving money
- Saving time
- Feeling secure
- Improving one's health
- Being more attractive
- Having a more youthful appearance
- Enjoying better sex
- Impressing others
- Being part of a special group
- Helping the family

When you sell something (even an idea), ask yourself, why should anyone buy it? For example, imagine you are selling sunglasses. You might ask yourself, why would anyone buy these sunglasses? The answer depends on whether the glasses are fashion accessories or only have the function of protecting the eyes. If they are fashion accessories, the benefit could be to impress others, demonstrate status, or be more attractive. At this point present this benefit using a story, such as research, a metaphor, or point out to them what they would miss out on if they did not buy your product. So the next time you are trying to convince someone or sell a product, try this formula.

Below, we will look at how to get people out of a negative state of mind.

How to get people out of negative moods

Have you tried to produce change in someone who is in a negative state of mind? You probably have, and you know how difficult, or impossible, it is to succeed. Fortunately, there is a language pattern that will help us change a person's state to a more positive one that allows them to see new possibilities. This is a very easy pattern to use and you only need two words that, despite their simplicity, have great power when used in the following way:

"(X) again. And this is because (y)"

In this pattern, (x) is the problem the person is facing. It is better for the person themselves to tell you how they are feeling than to try to read their thoughts and use your assumptions. The second part of this diagram, (y), is the reason why his or her state will change.

As you will see in the following diagrams, the word "why" is very powerful, since most people are easily persuaded to do something when they are given a reason to do it, even if it is a weak reason.

Let's look at some examples:

"I know you still can't understand it. And that's only because you need more examples."

"You still lack confidence. And that's only because you need more practice."

We can also add small variations:

"Yes, it sounds expensive. And that's because I haven't yet shown you how much value it will add to your practice."

"I know you are skeptical. And that's because I haven't yet shown you how it works."

With this language pattern, we are acknowledging the person's negative experience and giving them a reason "to" change.

The "anchor" word in this pattern is equally important, since we are assuming that its status will change, and this is especially useful in the context of sales. If you're selling something, you probably know that it's hard to get people out of inertia to get them to spend, but all you need is the "anchor" word.

"Still" implies that your possible client is still stuck in the past, that what they have done so far has not gone well and that their problems have not been solved, but it also suggests that what you are offering them is the solution.

Let's look at some examples:

"If you still continue to use Microsoft Word to create documents ..." (Maybe you are selling another type of software to process documents.)

"Are you still looking for your soulmate?" (For a dating service or a book about relationships.)

"Do you still use Yahoo! to do Internet searches?" (And then provide your reasons why they should not use Yahoo!)

Again, I advise you not to be rigid and use your creativity to apply this pattern during your conversations. Personally, I like to use it in the form of a question, as in the examples above, since our minds are programmed to answer questions. Do you agree with me?

Below we will look at another technique for provoking emotional states.

How to provoke emotional states at the right time

This interesting pattern combines a projection of the future with a determined command and a premise. You may not be able to understand it now, but it is a very powerful combination. The pattern is as follows:

"You will be <positive or negative emotional state> when I tell/show you ..."

The determined command comes after "You will be ..." and is a part of the emotional state. Let's look at some examples to be able to understand it better:

"You will be very happy when I tell you the price of this course."

"You'll be thrilled when you find out where I'm taking you tonight."

"You're going to go crazy when I tell you what I did ..."

People feel more motivated to do something once their emotions have been stimulated, especially if they are strong emotions, and this pattern in particular is ideal for stimulating these kinds of emotions.

With the following schema, you will feel your mind bubbling as you discover ways to insert ideas into people's minds.

CHAPTER 20:

INSERTING IDEAS INTO PEOPLE'S MINDS

I will now show a technique I discovered writers of advertisements use to get people who read them to start thinking the way they want. This language pattern is very powerful, although, interestingly, few NLP practitioners are familiar with it. It is used to insert ideas into people's minds. The pattern is as follows:

"Is <the question> (x)?"

(X) is something positive or negative that you want people to think or believe. This could be a simple question that can be answered with "yes" or "no," although it is better to formulate rhetorical questions that express your opinion in a disguised way, for example:

"Are Dobermans the best watchdogs for your home?"

"Are Dobermans the most dangerous dogs in the world?"

Using questions in this way, even if you can answer simply with "yes" or "no," you can create an assumption, especially if the person receiving the message has no knowledge about the topic. However, even if the person knows something about the topic in question, he or she may still be intrigued enough to want to read or learn more about your point of view regarding the topic in question.

You can create different variations of this pattern and ask questions like:

"Have you noticed that ...?"

"Did you realize that ...?"

"Can you believe ...?"

Let's look at some examples:

"Have you noticed that people who use NLP patterns are successful in all areas of their lives?"

"Are you aware that property prices in this neighborhood will go up in the next few years?"

"Did you know that it is increasingly difficult to find a job without a professionally written resume?"

The interesting thing about this pattern is that it doesn't matter what people answer. They may answer "yes" or "no," but you have sown your idea in their minds. Also, you can use this pattern as a piece of evidence for your messages, even if it is not real evidence. For example, imagine you have to sell a book to improve performance, and part of your work is about a breathing method to increase awareness and performance. You might say something like this:

"Have you noticed that Tiger Woods inhales deeply three times before taking a shot? Well, there is a reason for that ..."

Now it's your turn: Can you think of this pattern's applications in your personal and professional life?

With the following schema you will learn how to change the direction of people's thoughts.

CHAPTER 21:

THE ILLUSION OF FREEDOM AND CHOICE

People hate to feel manipulated, and almost always want to believe they have made the final decision. In Ericksonian hypnosis there is a pattern of language called "double constraint," which are phrases that offer two or more choices, but in reality it is always the same choice. For example, "You can fall into trance now or in the next few minutes."

There is also a technique called "But you are free to choose." More than forty psychological studies suggest that this technique can duplicate the chance that someone will respond affirmatively to your request, and it is very simple to use. You have to state your request and then make it clear that the other person can reject it. For example:

"<Request>, but you are free not to accept."

"<Request>, although of course you don't have to."

"<Request>, although you don't have to feel obligated."

As you can see, the language you use is not important, so much as stating again that the other person has a choice to make. It must be said that this technique works best in person, although it can also be effective via email or telephone.

There is a variation of this schema for occasions when someone who knows their options needs help in narrowing them down to make their choice easier. The beauty of this schema is that it allows you to appear impartial by suggesting the option that suits you best. The pattern is as follows:

"The way I see it, you have X options."

Technically, you are only presenting two options, but now you have the opportunity to show them in such a way as to favor your preferred choice. The trick is to leave your favorite choice last so that it stands out as clearly favored.

Let's look at an example:

Imagine that you are opening a business and are looking for someone to join your venture. You've already noticed someone and, from their profile, you know they would be the support you need to grow. So, you start by making a statement to establish a favorable scenario that makes the option you are going to propose stand out. It might go something like this:

"So currently you are doing a job you hate. You don't like it, the days seem endless, it keeps you away from your family, and the pay is not even close to what you would like. I've shown you a job opportunity and you like it, but you're not sure exactly what to do. The way I see it, you have three options. First, you could look for another job, fix your resume, send out applications, do interviews, and in the meantime stay employed, to perhaps find another employer who offers you a similar package and probably the same kind of work at the same salary. Alternatively, you could do nothing at all, stay exactly where you are, accept the current situation, and simply let this opportunity pass you by. Or, as a third option, you could try it, work in parallel with what you are doing now and see how far you can go. Of these three options, which one seems most convenient to you?"

Concluding with the question "Which one seems most convenient to you?" means that you have to choose between these three options. You have arranged everything in such a way that the option of finding a new job is laborious and will be discarded, and if you have managed to connect enough pain to the option of staying where they are, this option will also be discarded, so the only option left, the easiest and most convenient, is the one you want them to choose. You have arranged the options in such a way that the last one is the one that presents the path of least resistance.

So start by saying "You have X options" and end with "Which one seems best to you?" to see people effortlessly choose the one you want. Your goal is to become a decision catalyst, and this pattern of language leads to an almost instantaneous decision.

You have certainly succeeded many times in getting people interested in something; however, it is the final decision-making process that leads to the result, so you have to help them choose by creating easy options, and the easiest decisions are the polarized ones. Red wine or white wine? Beach or mountain?

Let's look at some examples, simplifying as much as possible the options that are presented to a person. Remember that your goal is to offer options by making one of them stand out as the easiest option.

"There are two kinds of people in this world: those who leave their economic success in the hands of their employees, and those who take full responsibility and build their own future. What kind of person are you?"

"There are two kinds of people in this world: those who judge something even before they try it and those who try it and base their opinion on their own experience. What kind of person are you?"

"There are two kinds of people in this world: those who oppose change in favor of nostalgia and those who stay with the times and create a better future. What kind of person are you?"

Now I want you to think that there are two kinds of people in this world: those who read this kind of book and do nothing and those who put into practice what they read and get immediate results. Below, we will see another variation of this schema that you can use to highlight the alternative that suits you best. The schema is called the decoy effect.

The decoy effect describes a situation in which you have three different possibilities, two of which are genuine and one of which is much worse in almost every other; that is, it is simply a decoy. Here is an example of three different possible subscriptions to *The Economist*:

Option 1: Online subscription. US$59 per year.

Option 2: Corporate subscription. US$125 per year.

Option 3: Corporate and online subscription. US$125 per year.

It is evident that subscription 2 is a decoy. No one is supposed to choose it (corporate subscription for $125), since for the same price you can get the corporate and online subscription.

Dan Ariely, professor of psychology and behavioral economics at Duke University, describes this example of *The Economist* in his book *Predictably Irrational*. During one study, Ariely had one hundred MIT students choose among the three previous options for subscribing to *The Economist*. The results were as follows:

Option 1: Sixteen students chose the first option (a subscription to Economist.com for $59 per year).

Option 2: Zero students chose the second option (a corporate subscription for $125 per year).

Option 3: Eighty-four students chose the third option (a corporate and online subscription for $125 per year).

Now, since no one chose the second option (corporate subscription only), what would happen if we eliminated it altogether?

Ariely eliminated the second option and presented the first and third options to one hundred other MIT students. Here's what happened:

Sixty-eight chose the first option (a subscription to Economist.com for $59 a year).

Thirty-two chose the third option (a corporate and online subscription for $125 per year).

The difference is significant. The elimination of the decoy option made the third option (corporate and online subscription) less attractive, leading people to decide to buy the cheaper option (online subscription only). However, when the decoy option was present, most students (84%) chose the more expensive subscription (corporate and online).

So if you present different options to your clients or anyone else you wish to influence, you can add a decoy option to highlight the option that is most convenient for you.

CHAPTER 22:

USING INTERNAL REPRESENTATIONS TO DIRECT THOUGHTS

Internal representations can force the direction of a person's thoughts toward what you are saying. This happens all the time naturally, but here you will learn what happens in a person's mind when you talk to them, and you will probably never have a normal conversation again.

If I were talking to you right now, your unconscious mind would have to create an internal representation of whatever I am saying in order for it to make sense. If you need to remember what an internal representation is, you can go back and look at the first part of this book, entitled *Basic Concepts of Neurolinguistic Programming*. Do you remember that? Very well, then let's continue. For example, if I say, "Pedro sees the mountain behind the house," you will have to create an internal representation of Pedro, a mountain and a house. Do you follow? Good. Now, if I say, "Pedro does not see the mountain behind the house, because Pedro, the mountain and the house do not exist," what do you think would happen in your mind?

Exactly! Your unconscious mind will have to create the same internal representation of the elements I named, even though I'm saying they don't exist. So in order for something to make sense, we always have to create an internal representation.

The following is a slightly more complex representation. Pay attention to the difference between the two sentences:

1. "Understanding this concept is difficult."
2. "Understanding this concept is not easy."

Both have the same logical meaning, but have a different representation. This is the fundamental idea of much of the patterns we have seen so far.

Now we can take this concept and use it to direct people's imaginations. When we use words such as "imagine," "consider," "suppose," or phrases such as "what if ...," "why don't ...," "think about ..." we are giving a direct command or instruction to people's minds to make them use their imagination the way we want them to think.

Can you understand how stealthy this technique is? Simply by saying the right things I can force your internal representations without leaving you any choice, unless you avoid listening to me or reading what I write. Consider all the power to influence you will have over people, and imagine the way you can get them to do more things for you with this new knowledge.

Consequently, if you are trying to influence a person, it is a good idea to know their preferred representational systems. For example, musicians tend to be more auditory. Chiropractors are more kinesthetic and landscape painters visual. But what happens when we don't know someone's preferred representational system?

Fortunately, we have a word we can use in this situation. You have probably seen it in countless numbers of effective advertisements. The word is "imagine."

This word automatically triggers the visualization process by simply naming it, and it is probably the most powerful communication tool we have, because it allows people to imagine any personal vision in their own minds and hearts.

The power of this word comes from the simple fact that it can evoke anything in the mind of the listener of the message, and what can be imagined is, as a result, infinitely personal. You don't need to tell people the details of what they need to imagine; simply encourage them to do so.

The clearest demonstration of this process is reading. When you read, you translate the black-and-white symbols on the page into sharp images in your mind, but each reader's mental images are different. This leads each reader to collaborate with the author in creating his or her own representation. Cinema, on the other hand, despite all its wonders, is an infinitely more passive medium and weakens the imagination instead of stimulating it.

In this sense, messages must say what people want to hear. The key to success in speech patterns is to personalize and humanize the message to provoke emotion. People will forget what you say, but they will never forget how you made them feel. If listeners can connect your message to their own life experiences, you will have succeeded in personalizing your message.

Advertisements do not sell products as a mere tool or as an item with a specific and limited use; rather, they sell the image of who you will be when you use that product. You will be a smarter, sexier, more attractive, more admired person. However, it is not about creating false expectations, as that would detract from credibility. It is about encouraging the recipient of the message to want something better and then giving it to them.

And what is the best way to get your message across?

Through visualization. You have to create a vivid image that the person can use. Misused visualization can ruin even the most popular ideas and products. Think of the makers of the Infiniti, arguably Nissan's best car in the past two decades: They made the wrong decision to launch this new model invisibly, literally. The launch of the Infiniti coincided exactly with that of Lexus, which was using an opposite strategy: a visual approach.

Lexus' traditional advertising campaign showed its new model traveling along a winding road while displaying the slogan "The relentless pursuit of perfection." Although it was not spectacular, it was a solid advertising campaign. In contrast, Infiniti did not want to use a slogan, or even show off its new car, while it decided to create nine advertisements intended to illustrate the fantasies of possible drivers. The "fantasy" campaign was based on a Japanese interpretation of luxury, almost spiritual in its depiction, as opposed to the literal interpretation of Western consumers, compromising the credibility and weight of the message.

While Lexus filled its advertisements with data about the "European luxury car tradition" and beautiful images of its new car, Infiniti's ads were deliberately vague, showing only clear skies, trees, rivulets of water, never showing a clear image of the car. Not a single one.

Nissan created a communication equation that was doomed to failure: a totally invisible advertising design with display-free ads. In the months that followed, Nissan spent more time defending its advertising campaign than launching its cars. The moral is this: thinking is literal, and if you can't see yourself doing something, the chances of you actually doing it are slim to none.

People make decisions based on the images they see in their minds, so if you can put images in their minds, you can use those images' results to influence their decisions.

But how can we create images in the minds of others?

It is very simple. It is done by telling a story. You probably remember that when you were a child you listened to many good stories that began with the words "Once upon a time ..."

When we heard those words, we knew it was time to relax, enjoy the moment and embrace our imagination as someone used the words to paint a magical world we could travel into. Now that we are adults, it would be a lot more difficult to create that same effect with the words "once upon a time," so we need a language pattern that can create the same visual result.

The pattern is as follows:

"Just imagine ..."

When we use "imagine" as an imperative (command or instruction) we are very likely to be able to engage a person's entire internal experience.

"Imagine what it will be like ..."

"Imagine for a moment what it will be like in a month ..."

"Now imagine ..."

"Imagine what you would do if ..."

"Just imagine how you would feel ..."

"What happens when you imagine ...?"

To make the most of this language pattern, at the end of the sentence you need to indicate the benefit of what you want people to do, and you can also indicate the consequences of not doing what you want others to do, although in general, it is more effective to create a focus from a positive point of view. For example:

"Just imagine what things will be like in six months, once you improve this."

"Just imagine what your family will say if you let this opportunity pass you by."

"Just imagine the look on your children's faces when they see you getting this."

"Just imagine the positive impact this decision could have."

"Imagine what your life will be like once you master this language pattern."

"Imagine for a moment what your routine will be like a month from now when you can persuade anyone using these techniques."

When the unconscious mind hears the word "imagine," it cannot avoid imagining and experiencing the scenario you are creating. Allow the power of the other person's mind to create a reality more vivid than anything you could ever describe.

Let people's minds do the hard work and imagine the big difference this simple language pattern will create in your personal and professional life.

Let's look at a particular application of this language pattern: how to ask for a pay raise.

How to ask for a raise or promotion

Most of us feel uncomfortable at the thought of going to the office of our boss to solicit a raise or promotion. It is one of the most hated conversations by most people so much that they prefer to put it off indefinitely. It is a situation that requires delicacy and diplomacy, strength and determination. The most important thing is to put yourself in your boss's shoes. To him or her, your pay raise or promotion is not a reward for what you have done so far, but a specific investment in your future commitment. The question your boss will ask is not "What has he or she done for me lately," but rather "What will he or she do for me tomorrow?"

Be prepared to explain how well you have done your job, but consider that demonstrating past and current value is only half the message you need to give. It will be more effective if you emphasize what your boss is most concerned about, that is, the next client, future contracts, the next project. Use the concept of consequences, but without threats or blackmail. No one likes to be cornered; on the contrary, this could easily lead to a negative response, a firm "no."

You must consider that the focus of your boss's decision will not be that you "deserve" a raise, but that there will be certain implied consequences if you are not given one. You have already demonstrated your value; now you need to focus your efforts on convincing your boss to make sure that they imagine what would happen if that value were not there.

"Imagine if ..." are the two most effective words you can use in this situation. "Imagine if I had not worked on project X." "Imagine if I had not closed contract X last week." By simply taking your boss through a little thought experiment, you will create a subtle but clear vision of not being able to achieve your own work goals.

If you can make the visualization produced by the "imagine if" language pattern demonstrate your future value, you are likely to get that raise, bonus, or promotion. Of course, some bosses use raises to reward previous efforts, but "imagine if" is the best trick for those who do not.

Below, we will look at another language pattern that uses people's internal representations. The pattern is "How would you feel if ...?"

How would you feel if ...?

If you want people to do things they normally do not want to do, you must first find an honest reason that is strong enough for them; but to understand which reasons are powerful enough, you must first understand how people motivate themselves.

All actions taken by people are motivated by these two factors: to avoid a potential loss or to gain a potential gain. That is, they either want to get closer to the light, or they want to get away from what could hurt them. Interestingly, in the real world, people put much more effort into avoiding a potential loss than they put into acquiring a potential gain.

But that is not all. In addition to understanding people's true motivation, you also need to know whether they base their decisions on emotion or logic, although mostly, people make decisions emotionally and then justify them with logic; that is, something has to give a positive feeling before it makes sense to us.

Surely you have felt confused after having a conversation with someone who did not follow your advice, and you may have thought, "I don't know why they don't do what I told them, even when my advice makes complete sense." If you try to make your arguments prevail because your advice makes sense, you are trying to persuade someone for the wrong reasons. People make decisions based on what they like, and if you can give them that feeling, the rest is easy.

By presenting a future scenario with the language pattern "How will you feel if ...?" you allow the other person to time travel to the desired moment and imagine the relative emotions that will be created at that time. In other words, with this language pattern you create a scenario of future-related conditions that others can see and feel.

Let's look at some examples:

"How would you feel if this decision brought you a promotion in your job?"

"How would you feel if the competition overtook you?"

"How would you feel if you changed this?"

"How would you feel if you lost everything?"

"How would you feel if you were free of doubts next year, living in your dream home and planning your next vacation?"

So by creating possible future scenarios with this language pattern you can get people excited, giving real reasons for them to achieve what they want, or to move away from what they don't want, and the greater the contrast between what they want and what they don't want, the more likely they will act.

CHAPTER 23:

CREATING A PERSPECTIVE OF DOUBT

On what frequency do you find yourself in conversations that quickly become a debate because you are talking to someone who thinks they know better and, perhaps, also wants to lecture you on their opinions?

To influence others, you must be aware of how to control a conversation and regain control by destabilizing the other person's position from a perspective of certainty to one of doubt.

In general, people instinctively try to create this position of uncertainty by directly questioning the other person's opinion, and sometimes even arguing. Surely you have had times when you have felt frustrated when someone failed to understand what you were saying and for not being able to overcome their preconceived notions. This happens regularly when you try to introduce new ideas or concepts, and the other person has the kind of "know it all" mentality that, in many cases, can be difficult to overcome.

The best way to overcome a "know it all" mentality is to question the knowledge on which the other person's opinion is based; that is, the goal is to convert the situation to one in which the other person admits that his or her opinion is based on insufficient evidence, while at the same time retaining the ability to remain in conversation. To achieve this goal, we use the following schema:

"What do you know about ...?"

This pattern is a slight threat to the other person's knowledge base and forces them to share the parameters on which their arguments are based, which often causes them to realize that their strong opinion was unfounded.

Let's look at some examples:

"What do you know about our work and the way we do things?"

"What do you know about all the things that have changed since (insert event)?"

"What do you know about how things really work here?"

"What do you know about the benefits of ...?"

These questions allow the other person to realize that his or her opinion is not necessarily right, and he or she can quickly move on to being much more perceptive to the change, as long as you do not behave aggressively in the way you ask questions, since when we are asked questions, we quickly become defensive. If you apply this pattern correctly, the worst thing that could happen is to become aware of the true basis of the other person's argument, at which point you can express your own opinion. Use this pattern to challenge others with confidence, respect, and avoid arguments, which always end up with everyone losing since, when it comes to persuasion, either everyone wins or everyone loses.

Below we will look at another schema that will allow you to create a new perspective.

CHAPTER 24:

CREATING A POSITIVE PERSPECTIVE

These language patterns provide you with a tool to convert a negative perception into a positive one using a technique called a label. It is the acceptance of this new label that creates the ability to change the direction of a conversation with minimal effort and leads to a more positive outcome.

The pattern is as follows:

"The good news is ..."

By using these words before you lay out your ideas, you will ensure that the recipient accepts the label you have added so that this optimistic turn can help them deal with the negativity in their life, keep them from ending up in a conversation full of guilt and self-compassion, and help them look in a new direction.

For example, if one of your friends is not sure if he or she has the skills needed to successfully perform the new position to which he or she has been promoted, you might say, "The good news is that I can recommend an ideal training course for this position, and you can complete it at your own pace to get all the skills you need to succeed in this new challenge."

What happens when someone opposed to change says they want to be more successful? In this case you might respond with, "The good news is that you already know that what you're doing now hasn't worked the way you wanted, so what would you lose by trying this new alternative?"

As you can see, this pattern of language makes people change their perspective and look forward with optimism, removing any negative energy from the conversation, a skill that is especially useful not only when you want to achieve something, but also when you simply want to help someone see new possibilities.

Below we will look at a surprising method of persuasion that has proven to be extremely effective.

CHAPTER 25:

THE MOST EFFECTIVE, ALBEIT INEXPENSIVE, METHOD OF INFLUENCING

A little-known persuasion technique called "disrupt-then-reframe" (DTR) has proven to be very effective, and it is important for you to be familiar with it at this point. However, I must warn you: the DTR technique is more of a cheap (though very effective) trick than an actual technique, and some may consider it morally questionable.

The study described below is one that initiated this field of research. Davis and Knowles (1999) demonstrated the effectiveness of the DTR technique by selling greeting cards door-to-door for a local charity, and they used two different strategies.

Strategy 1: In the "normal" condition, they told people that the price was $3 for every eight tickets. In this way they were able to achieve a sale in 40 percent of homes.

Strategy 2: In the DTR condition, first they said the price was 300 cents for every eight tickets, and immediately afterward they said, "It's a bargain!" In this way they were able to make sure that they sold their tickets in 80 percent of the houses.

This is a big achievement for a small change in words, but how and why does it work?

The DTR technique works because first of all it interrupts normal thought processes. In this case, people's attention is distracted as they try to process that enigmatic "300 cents" and find out why someone says the price in cents instead of dollars. After the interruption there is rephrasing, in this case, the words "It's a bargain!" While people are distracted by the price in cents (for a second or two), they are more likely to simply accept the suggestion that the tickets are a bargain.

Interruption only works for a few seconds, so rephrasing must be done immediately, before the person's critical faculties come back on, so you have to make sure that the interruption is slightly confusing, and not completely unintelligible.

Many may wonder if this effect was timely, and whether it would work in other cases, but the DTR technique has been tested in fourteen different studies with hundreds of participants (Carpenter and Boster, 2009) and has been shown to increase charitable donations, animate people to complete surveys and change their attitudes. It is also surprisingly effective in sales situations where people normally do not trust this kind of deception. So, even if you don't want to use this technique, it is useful for you to be familiar with it.

If a salesperson says something confusing ("New car, new woman") and then hits you with their persuasive phrase ("Between you and me, this car is an amazing deal"), be sure to take some time before deciding. It is amazing that such a simple manipulation has the power to confuse us.

CHAPTER 26:

HOW TO MAKE SURE YOUR SUGGESTIONS ARE ACCEPTED

This technique is known as "using compound suggestions," and it is based on the principle of consistency that you learned in the second part of the book. We will do everything we can to maintain a consistent image of ourselves. In this regard, research has shown that once a suggestion has been accepted by the unconscious mind, it becomes easier for additional suggestions to be accepted as well.

The process is very simple. You just have to say something that the other person is very likely to agree with, and then you have to add the suggestion that you want to implant.

The structure is this:

<Suggestions, facts or opinions easily accepted> + <What you want the other person to think or do>

Let's look at some examples:

"You are resting comfortably in that chair. It would be nice to go into a deep trance state."

"Knowing how to communicate effectively is vital to business, isn't it? Your company needs to take part in this seminar to meet this challenging time."

"To be successful in any area of life, it is essential to have the ability to influence and persuade people. And to do this, it is important to have a specific method. This book on speech patterns contains that method."

This language pattern is very simple and easy to master. There is no need to expand on it, so we will immediately move on to the next one, in which you will learn how to appeal to people's identities.

CHAPTER 27:

APPEALING TO PEOPLE'S IDENTITY

One of the most powerful ways to persuade a person is to appeal to their identity: who they are, who they want to be or who they don't want to be. In his famous book *How to Make Friends and Influence People*, Dale Carnegie says that we must give others a reputation that they absolutely want to maintain, and the course of history has shown that he was indeed right. There are many ways to do this, and below we will look at a very simple and effective language pattern.

The pattern is as follows:

"I can tell you that you are a person <identity> because <reason why>"

Examples:

"I can tell you are a very intelligent person because you are reading this book."

"I can tell you that you are a person who does not want to be part of the masses, because you are now reading this."

"I know you are a person who has high standards, because otherwise you wouldn't be here."

If you have read this book in order, you will remember that the word *why* is a very powerful means of persuasion, even if the reason does not make much sense. This is because we are "programmed" to respond to the word "because." This pattern is fantastic, since it appeals to the person's identity and makes him or her part of a desired group, another great tool of persuasion, as we saw in the second part of the book, which depends on the need for affiliation.

One variation of the pattern is to use the words "open mind." If you asked a room with a hundred people which of them considered themselves open-minded, surely more than ninety hands would be raised. Almost all of us respond to this criterion, and it is quite easy to see why. Remember the "illusion of freedom and choice" schema? In this case, we create a polarized perception of choice, and when you think that the other alternative is to have a "closed mind," this virtually forced choice will guide most people toward your idea.

Let us look at some examples of the application of this schema:

"Is your mind open enough to try this new alternative?"

"Do you have an open enough mind to give them a chance?"

"Is your mind open enough to increase your monthly income using this method?"

"Is your mind open enough to consider working together?"

By expressing options in this way, it is very difficult for the other person to reject your idea and, at the very least, you force them to consider the possibility.

Now let's look at another way to appeal to people's identity. This schema is probably one of my favorites because it helps build a basis of agreement quickly and easily on which we can rest the following persuasive messages. It is worth saying that this technique is much more powerful during a conversation with a stranger than with someone you already know.

The pattern is as follows:

"I bet you're a little like me."

As we saw in the previous diagram ("How to get your suggestions accepted"), my experience has taught me that when you get people to agree first, it is more difficult for them to disagree later. Let's look at an example:

Imagine being afraid that someone might object to your idea because you don't have time to demonstrate its benefits. At the beginning of the conversation you might say something like ...

"I bet you're a little like me and you like to work hard now, knowing that you will get the fruits of what you do today."

"I bet you're a bit like me and you hate watching television in the evening because you'd rather devote yourself to something profitable."

"I bet you're a little like me and you're a busy person who's always jumping through hoops to get everything done."

If you use these kinds of statements in early conversations, while maintaining eye contact with the other person, when you see him or her nodding you will know that he or she agrees with these concepts, and that is the signal that indicates that it will be very difficult for him or her to object to your following ideas.

Now, to conclude this outline, let me ask you one thing: Is your mind open enough to try this language pattern?

CHAPTER 28:

HOW TO CHANGE OR WEAKEN BELIEFS

The following is an eleven-step technique for easily changing negative beliefs to powerful beliefs. It is an advanced NLP technique that uses the concept of conditioning that you learned in the first part of the book, so I recommend that you read it quickly to get an idea of how it works and then, when you want to apply it, go back and read it again carefully. As with most NLP techniques, you can use it on yourself as well as on others. So, first we will look at how to apply it on yourself and then we will adapt these concepts so that you can use them on others.

Let's start then.

Step 1: Think of a limiting belief that is causing you pain or causing you to stop doing something you should be doing. Think about one of your goals and what is preventing (mentally) you from achieving it. For example, "I know I should exercise more, but I think the exercise might hurt me, so I'd rather not do it."

Step 2: Think of a powerful belief that is opposite to the negative belief you identified in the previous step. What would you like to believe? Continuing with the example, "With regular exercise I will become stronger, more attractive, and I will be less likely to get hurt." Clearly, this is a more positive and healthy belief.

Step 3: Think of something you would never do, such as pushing a person in front of a bus, locking your finger in the door, or sticking a cigarette in your ear. Something that generates a strong reaction of "NO, NEVER!" Really feel it inside you.

Step 4: Break this state. Get up, walk around for a while and clear your mind.

Step 5: Think of something you would absolutely love, such as being a millionaire, a buffet of your favorite food, or making love. At this point you want to generate a strong reaction of "ABSOLUTELY YES!" Keep thinking about it until you really feel this feeling in your whole body.

Step 6: Break the state again. Get up, walk for a few moments and clear your mind.

Step 7: Focus on your negative beliefs, and as you do so, remember the emotion of that strong NO! Really feel it, that NO! and associate it with your negative belief. Carry out this step several times.

Step 8: Break the state again.

Step 9: Now think about your powerful positive belief. As you think about how great it will be to have this new belief in your life, relive the feeling of that powerful ABSOLUTELY YES! In other words, as you think about the positive belief, say (mentally or out loud) ABSOLUTELY YES!

Step 10: Break the state again.

Step 11: Try it and project yourself into the future. Think about both beliefs and see if they look different. Has the negative belief become weaker? Has the positive one become stronger?

Now think about tomorrow, next week, next month, next year. What do you feel your life will be like with this new empowering belief?

Conditioning techniques are very powerful when done correctly, and below you will learn how you can covertly implement a shorter version of this technique to change the beliefs of others.

Michael Hall, one of the pioneers of the practical application of NLP, uses this technique on his clients. Suppose you are talking to a friend, single, who is afraid to approach women he likes and you want to help him overcome this block.

The first thing you need to do is to generate a strong response of "NO!" and to do that you will say phrases like, "I bet you like being alone, eating dinner alone, waking up alone every day and not seeing anyone ..." "I think you like not having anyone to hug and share your life with ..." "I bet you'd like to be alone on your deathbed with no one around, wouldn't you?"

Then you will have to generate a strong "YES!" response, and to do so you will say phrases such as, "Would you like to have a special woman in your life?" "Can you imagine how great it would be to meet your soul mate?" "It's easy to think about how wonderful life would be if you met a good mate, don't you think?"

Usually, these questions are already enough to change people's behavior or beliefs. However, from this point, you will be in a better position to persuade your friend or help him or her take new actions, which will be even more positive. So now it's your turn to think: What actions would you like your friend to take? That he go on a blind date? For him to ask that girl he met at work on a date? What do you think his objections to this idea would be? Which technique, among those we have learned so far, would you use to persuade him? How would you lay out the alternatives he has so that he would choose the one you want?

Take a moment and think about this scenario. Try to work it out. Mentally review what you have learned so far and try to devise a possible strategy to persuade your friend. The only way to master what you have learned is to use this knowledge. Don't be afraid to be wrong. Play with what you know. I could go on and on writing to try to solve everything for you, but we know that would not help you. You already have the knowledge you need; now you have to think and apply it.

But we are not done yet. We still have a pattern left to learn. Below, we will learn how to "open" people's mindsets.

CHAPTER 29:

HOW TO "OPEN" PEOPLE'S MINDSETS

Sometimes all you need for someone to change their opinion is just a little leverage. This leverage can be achieved by using a "modal possibility operator" and an almost impossible task. Sounds complicated? Read on and you will understand better.

The language pattern is as follows:

"If I did <impossible task>, would you be willing to listen?"

The impossible task can be anything from guessing a number from one to a hundred to what song will play next on the radio. It doesn't matter. What matters is that you will have gotten a deal, which shows that there is a part in the other person that is willing to change.

Another popular technique is what is known as "the foot in the door." As its name implies, the foot-in-the-door technique gets a person to agree to a big request by first making a small request. In other words, you start by getting a small "yes" and then get a bigger "yes." This works because of the principle of consistency that we learned in the second part of the book. (If you don't remember it, it's a good idea to go back and read it again.)

A particularly representative study to test this technique was carried out by a team of psychologists who telephoned a group of housewives and asked if they could answer some questions about the different products they used.

Then, half a week later, the psychologists called again to ask for a two-hour evaluation of the products they had in their homes, which would take place by sending five or six men to their homes and opening all the cupboards and places where they kept those products. What was the result? The researchers found that those women were twice as likely to agree to a "raid" on their home than the housewives who only received the largest request.

The foot-in-the-door technique is illustrated very well with a couple of stories. The first one, called "The Cookie and the Mouse," can be summarized as follows:

Once upon a time there was a child who gave a mouse a cookie. At that point, the mouse asked for a glass of milk. Then, the mouse also wanted a straw to drink the milk, so it asked for one. Wishing to avoid walking around with milk-stained whiskers, the mouse asked for a mirror. When it stood in front of the mirror, it decided to cut its hair, so it asked for a pair of nail scissors. Later, to sweep away its trimmed hair, the mouse asked for a broom. Feeling a little tired, at that point the mouse wanted them to read it a story, take a nap, draw a picture, and hang the picture on the refrigerator. The sight of the refrigerator made the mouse thirsty, so it asked for a glass of milk. And at that point the mouse wanted a cookie to eat along with the milk, starting the cycle all over again once more.

The following story, in which a variation of the foot-in-the-door technique is used, is known as "The Stone Soup," by George Patton. The Stone Soup is an old folk tale about a wanderer who traveled through a village during a famine that had broken out after the war. The shortage of food had caused all the villagers to hide and jealously preserve what they had so when the wanderer went from door to door asking for something to eat, he received nothing. At that point, the wanderer decides to adopt a different strategy. He takes out of his sack a large iron pot and a stone. He fills it with water, boils it and throws in the stone. The villagers, curious, ask him what he is doing. "I am making stone soup," the wanderer replies.

The wanderer says that he had once tried stone soup with carrots, which was delicious. At that point he asks if he could have some carrots to add to the soup, so as to give it some flavor. One of the villagers, who is very curious, goes to find a carrot and gives it to him for his stone soup.

At that point the wanderer recounts that he once tasted stone soup with some onions, and he says, "Oh, boy, that was the best stone soup I ever tasted." At that point he asks the villagers for some onions, and the villagers, curious, go looking for onions. The story continues with the wanderer asking for more ingredients, adding potatoes, tomatoes, bread and meat to the soup. Eventually, the wanderer pulls the original stone out of the pot without being seen, and the actual soup remains.

The moral of the story is, in a way, similar to that of the cookie and the mouse, but what does Patton have to do with this tale?

Legend says that after hearing this story, General George Patton, one of the most prominent generals of World War II, was inspired to use a similar technique during the period when he was ordered to defend instead of attack.

Patton, annoyed at being ordered to maintain an "aggressive defense" instead of attacking directly with most of his forces, complied with what he was told, but ordered a tank reconnaissance. Obviously, reinforcements were needed to accompany the tanks and, as a result, progressively more forces were needed. In the end, an entire Third Army Corps was involved in the reconnaissance mission, just what Patton wanted. So if you have a big request and you need someone to fulfill it, you can increase your chances of success if you first get a smaller request accepted, and this is because of the principle of consistency.

Now we will look at a technique that is practically the opposite, and is known as "the door in the face." It works like this: you have to make a large request that you expect to be rejected by the person you are addressing, and then make a more moderate and reasonable request that will be more likely to be accepted.

The name "door in the face" refers to the large initial request that will most likely be rejected, like a door metaphorically slammed in the face.

One study that sought to demonstrate the effectiveness of the door-in-the-face technique divided participants into two groups. The first group was asked to volunteer to spend two hours a week counseling juvenile offenders for two years (major request). After the request was declined, they were asked to accompany those juvenile offenders on a trip to the zoo for one day (minor request). Participants in the second group received only the minor request.

What were the results? Fifty percent of participants in the first group agreed with the minor request compared to 17 percent in the second group.

This technique is based on our natural tendency to have more confidence in the first piece of information we get when we make a decision. And this, when we talk about persuasion, is called "conditioning." For example, imagine walking into a used car showroom and seeing a car similar to the one you are looking for at $10,000. When the salesperson tries to sell you a car that costs $7,000, it seems like a reasonable, almost cheap price, even when it continues to be a higher price than the car's true value. This is because a conditioning has been established, and consequently you judge everything by that parameter.

This is what makes the door-in-the-face technique so effective. Once conditioning has been established with the initial, larger request, the second, smaller request seems more reasonable and moderate.

This is the last pattern we will look at individually. Below, you will learn how to use these patterns through scripts, and then we will see how to convert scripts into conversations.

CHAPTER 30:

PATTERNS TO SPEED UP YOUR PROCESS

The truth about all these language patterns is that there is no one magic pattern that automatically gives you the results you want, and what makes them work is that you have a process and sequence of patterns that direct people to the results you want.

You need to have an arsenal of speech patterns that you can use naturally in your conversations, and that's what we're going to deal with now. So far we've looked at the patterns separately, but now we're going to start putting the pieces together so that you can create your own persuasive pattern sequences.

In this lesson we will focus on combining patterns into a few paragraphs and scripts so that later, in the following lesson, we can use them in more elaborate conversations. The idea is to get your mind used to thinking strategically about persuasion and how to influence without it having to worry about specific language patterns.

At this point, some may think that they cannot see the importance of scripts and would rather practice directly within the flow of a conversation. If you think so, I might also agree, and the point of the chapter is not to memorize scripts, but to learn how persuasive language works to build a library of useful phrases in your mind and then practice in a real-world context. Using this approach, you will quickly learn to integrate patterns, which will become a natural part of your language, and you will also begin to think strategically to apply complete sequences of patterns.

So now let's look at a strategic approach. I want you to start thinking about the sequence of internal representations through which you are going to travel your "subject." As you know by now, we use the term *subject* or *potential client* indiscriminately in this book to refer to the person you want to persuade.

Let's say you're writing a sales pitch for a personal development course you've just prepared and you've already bombarded several subjects with a huge amount of course benefits, but you haven't achieved the desired effect. What can you do now?

Let's look at a possible sequence of patterns through which you could run the subject:

1. Generate interest /anticipation
2. Recognizing needs
3. Establish the benefits that would result from meeting the needs, including a vision of the future with greater benefits
4. Enthusiasm to meet those needs

Please note that this is not a real sales process, but just a way to think about the emotional journey you will make the person experience. So if we add a little more detail, the structure of the conversation should look like this:

1. You will make a brief report about another person who is achieving incredible results (only the result, not the way he or she achieved it), and you will conclude with a sentence like "What would you like to achieve?"
2. You will ask presuppositional questions about what prevents the subject from achieving his or her goal and the implications of remaining in the same situation.

3. You will utter sentences about visions of the future related to having the tools that will enable them to do things differently and how this would improve their situation, in the future.
4. You will associate all these feelings with the product or idea you are presenting.

Very good, now process that for a moment. Think of a particular situation in your life where you want to convince someone to do or buy something.

Have you done it?

Remember that the only way to internalize and learn new information is by applying it to cases in your real life. I could come up with the most innovative examples to present this information to you, but if you don't internalize it, in a few days you will have forgotten it.

Well, let's continue with the example. Let's develop the script a little more so that you can get a complete idea:

1. Have you met Andrea yet? She was able to realize her dream of traveling and filming documentaries around the world. She was even sponsored by a sports brand. This past week she was in the Sahara Desert. It is unbelievable that the only thing she needed was to think about her dreams, to realize them.
2. Wouldn't it be great if you too could make your dreams come true? If you could do that, which dream would you make come true? What is important to you about ...? (Insert your answer here.) I don't know if you've thought about it yet, but it's been since you were young that you've always had all these plans, dreams, ambitions, and as you've grown up, you're still not on the road to getting the things you want. What is stopping you now from running after your dreams? (At this point you have to increase negative feelings,

such as coming to the end of life with unrealized ambitions, imagining the last moment of life and thinking about all the things that could have been, etc. Do this carefully and don't go too deep, as we all prefer happy thoughts.)

3. All it took for Andrea was just a small change in her thinking and she started doing the things she had always wanted to do but did not know how. Amazingly, she was able to leave behind all her fears and mistakes. You too can change your beliefs, increase your self-confidence and motivate yourself to do those things you've always wanted (Note well the change from "Andrea" to "you." It seems obvious, but your subject will not notice it.) How would you feel if you could leave your past behind and embrace the future so that you could do the things you have always wanted? (Emphasize this point as much as possible, and probably the best way to do this is with questions ... How would you feel? What would you do? What would you say?)
4. Anyway, we are not talking about Andrea being able to achieve magnificent results, but the point is that you too can learn to do the same. Would you like me to tell you the name of the course in which Andrea learned to change her mindset so that she could achieve this?

You may have noticed that this is not a sales script. It is just an emotional journey for your subject and some ideas on how to use language. You can make this script much more complex if you think about the objections that might arise, and if you already know your subject, you can integrate their language and interests into your speech.

At this point it is time to think about process and mental practices. The goal now is to think in terms of sequences of internal representations and how persuasive language dovetails with all this.

Below, we will take the script you have just learned and convert it into a persuasive conversation.

CHAPTER 31:

MOVING FROM MONOLOGUES TO PERSUASIVE CONVERSATIONS

Until now we have learned independent language patterns and seen a script or monologue. But the reality is much more complex. Sometimes you only need to plant the seed of a thought in the other person's mind to get him or her to do what you want but, in general, persuasion is not a monologue but a two-way process involving both parties. In a conversation, the other person must have the opportunity to speak and, as a result, we must be able to connect our own schemas with what is being said. However, this part of the persuasion process need not be complex and, in fact, is one of the simplest, since it takes advantage of the knowledge we have already acquired.

By now we should be able to think on another level and begin to be aware of the sequences of other people's internal representations, the emotional journey by which we put them through, and the specific outcomes we want. In other words, you should manage the conversation, and a good mental process for doing that is as follows:

1. Inform: Formulating a sentence.

2. Invite: Ask for a response.

3. Knowledge: Make sure the other party knows you are listening.

For example:

– Inform: "Gabriel always throws good parties."

– Invite: "How did you meet him?"

– Knowledge: "I met him at work."

– Inform: "Gabriel told me that he works for a very good company."

– Invite: "What do you do specifically?"

– Knowledge/inform/invite: "It's an interesting job; you were lucky. How did you get it?"

And so on. This is a typical conversation, and you might ask why I am dividing it into separate parts. The answer is that I need to separate the parts so that we can insert different scripts while maintaining the flow. Now let's go through the conversation again, but this time let's add some changes in states and language patterns.

Remember how in the previous example I started the conversation by saying, "Gabriel always throws good parties"? This time I will start in a different way:

"It is always a pleasure when Gabriel invites me to one of his parties, because I know you will meet interesting people."

Certainly the first thing you will notice is the change in the referential index. I went from talking about myself to talking about you. Now let's continue with the example and see some other specific commands that I normally use. I will highlight them so that you can easily recognize them.

– Inform: "How did you meet Gabriel?"

– Knowledge: "From what I've been told, it must be a great place to work."

– Inform: "It seems to be a place where you find a lot of pleasant people. I like places where you can get excited and passionate about what you do."

– Invite: "What do you do? What are you really passionate about?"

– Knowledge: "I hadn't noticed how satisfying it can be."

– Inform: "I remember reading that passion, like any other emotional state, takes time to reach its fullest expression. For me_it is a slow process. When I see something for the first time, I think I'm going to enjoy it; then I start thinking about the things about it that interest me and the feeling starts in my stomach and gets more and more intense, until I end up acting impulsively."

It's pretty simple, don't you think? Things don't have to be complicated to be effective. All you have to do in a conversation is be aware of where you are and use that to build the next point. Start practicing in everyday conversations, but first let me give you some advice: Focus first on mastering the three-step process (inform, invite, know) to guide the conversation, before trying to insert language patterns. Notice how, with a little practice, you can steer a conversation naturally. I assure you that within a few days you will be familiar with the process, start adding some patterns, and notice the reactions you get. Eliminate all expectations and see what happens. The idea is to play, practice, and as you build your library of patterns, you will automatically begin to steer conversations in the direction you want.

Next, I will show you a version of my particular sales process with explanations of some elements of NLP. I hope that by reading my process you can create your own ideas and understand how you can integrate the different elements you have learned. Although it is focused on sales, you can adapt it to a generic persuasion process if you wish and, in fact, it will be an excellent exercise if you take this knowledge and try to apply it to a particular situation in your life.

Persuasion begins from the moment I say the first word to my subject. Do you agree with that? Well, I don't. It all starts before I even meet the potential client. Before I even say a word, I have to make sure I have the right mindset, so I use perceptual postures to get into their mind and understand the way they think. In this exercise, I imagine myself as being my subject, whether it is a group of people, an individual or an organization. Obviously, the more you know, the easier and more effective it will be to put it into practice, but even if I have no idea who the people involved are, I always take this step. The reason is that in this way my subconscious mind tries to think as others do. In this exercise I try to understand their beliefs, values, problems and benefits within the context of what I want them to do. Basically, I build rapport before I even meet them and, believe me, this helps tremendously in the context of persuasion.

Therefore, I ask myself some questions:

Do I know my product from the perspective of the potential customer?

What problems does it have or need to solve?

What results can you expect?

How should I articulate the benefits of my product to make them meaningful to my subject?

With that in mind, it's time to start the meeting. At this point I need to build trust through the patterns we have seen in this book. I always try to start a meeting by focusing it on the points of agreement, and if there is no agreement, I use the "structures of agreement" language pattern to agree with everything and at the same time maintain my opinions. Do you remember that?

It is important to offer, from the beginning, an incentive for the person to be interested in continuing the conversation. Normally, people do not invest their time in something they cannot benefit from. I don't necessarily mean an economic benefit, but it could simply be a pleasant moment. In the case of sales, it is very easy, since people like to get things for free, but regardless of what you offer, I always use language patterns to create anticipation and expectation.

During the conversation I ask questions to find the needs of the potential client and understand how he or she represents his or her world. Obviously, the questions I ask are based on the specific context of each situation, but here are some questions I normally use in the context of selling personal development courses:

"How do you see yourself in five years?"

"How much confidence do you have in that?"

"What skills, abilities, and mindset should you have to increase your chances of achieving your goal?"

"What will happen if you don't get these changes?"

"What benefits will it give you?"

"Why is it important that you get this?"

"What value do these new beliefs and mindsets have for you that will enable you to achieve your goals?"

Observe the sequence of these questions and also note that they are presuppositional. They are specifically in that order, so that the perspective moves from identifying the subject's goals to thinking about the consequences of achieving or not achieving these goals or needs.

If the person does not have a goal, a need, or does not associate the solution with a value greater than my price, it is better for them to go away and keep looking, because they will not be my customer.

The next step is to combine my solutions with your needs.

Once my potential client is aware of his or her needs and recognizes the value of meeting those needs, I present my course as a solution.

When you study NLP, this can seem a bit complicated, and I understand, because I've been there myself. Many practitioners will start talking through speech patterns, conditioning positive emotions to their product and negative states to their competitors' product, using different NLP techniques, and so on. I personally think it is not necessary to complicate things. The beauty is in the simplicity, and I think if you ask the questions in a meaningful sequence, according to what you learned in this book, and also present your solutions in a meaningful way, you can keep things simple and get the results you want.

This does not mean that one should avoid using advanced NLP techniques at all costs, it just means that my experience has shown me that if I stick to the basic fundamentals, everything else will be fine, but if I have made mistakes on the basics, even the most advanced NLP techniques will not work.

Let's look below at how to deal with one of the biggest obstacles when it comes to persuasion: objections.

CHAPTER 32:

DEALING WITH OBJECTIONS

Objections are part of everyday life. We face indecision from others in our personal and professional lives and, often, we have to resign ourselves to accepting the other person's idea; otherwise, certain conversations can turn into confrontations.

To overcome an objection, we must first understand what an objection is. The first key concept is to understand that an objection is simply a way of postponing the decision to another day, and not necessarily an absolute "no." The second key concept we need to understand is that when an objection is presented, there is a shift in the control of the conversation, and it is the person raising the objection who takes control, so you are obliged to abide by his or her wishes or walk away.

To be successful in our attempts at persuasion, we must maintain control of the conversation. The person in control is always the person asking the questions, so it is possible to quickly regain control responding with another question by treating every objection as nothing more than a question.

For example, some common objections are ...

"I don't have time."

"This is not the right time."

"I have no money right now."

"I need to talk to someone else before making this decision."

When you receive such an objection, the worst thing you can do is to respond with a counter-argument and make statements that refute the other person's opinion. The best way to deal effectively with each of these objections is to ask a question in the opposite direction.

Of course, you could develop unique and precise questions to challenge each objection you face, but the beauty of this language pattern is that it uses a generic question. The pattern is as follows:

"What makes you say that?"

This change of control forces the other person to give a response to fill in the gaps in their previous statement and explain what they really mean. It also prevents you from expressing bias or entering into an argument, and helps you better understand his or her point of view before recommending a next thought or action. This leaves you in a position where you can think better about your next moves or at least have a better understanding of why you disagree at this time.

Let us now take a look at another very effective schema that you can use immediately to get results when we face objections. It consists of asking a very direct question.

"What do I have to say or do for you to do (x)?"

Where (x) is what you want the other person to do.

This question is actually a thought process. The function of this question is to allow you to discover the criteria the person needs to do what you want.

You may be asking yourself, "But what if I don't like the answer?"

The truth is that the answer doesn't matter. The important thing here is that you have opened a possibility of agreement in the other person's subconscious mind because you are assuming that there is something you can do.

For example, in a dating conversation:

"What do I have to do to get an appointment?"

"We're not going on a date because I don't like you physically."

"I agree that I am not physically attractive, but the issue is not how I look, but how much fun we will have together."

In a sales conversation:

"What do I have to say to make you want to buy the product today?"

"You should say I can take it for free."

"The problem is not the cost of the product, but how much it will cost you not to have it. What do you need me to do to make you realize how much money you are losing by not buying the product?"

Therefore, as you can see, the goal of dealing with objections is not to take "no" for an answer. Let's look at another schema to accomplish this.

Imagine you ask for a favor and get a resounding "no." What do you do?

According to two experiments conducted by Boster and his colleagues, you should ask "Why not?" and then try to deal with the objections (Boster et al., 2009). The key is to turn the "no" of a resounding rejection into an obstacle to overcome. According to the theory, if you can deal with the obstacle, you are more likely to be granted what you ask for. For future reference, we will call this technique the "Why not?" technique.

Boster and his colleagues tested the "Why not?" technique by comparing it with the following established methods for getting what you want from a request (you will recognize that these are two methods you have already learned):

Door-in-the-face (DITF): First you make a very big request that is likely to be rejected. This is where the metaphorical door is slammed in your face. However, you immediately continue with a much smaller request that, in comparison, seems very reasonable. This has been shown to substantially increase the acceptance of the request.

Placebo information (IP): this technique is when you give someone a reason to do something, even if it is not a good reason; for example, it is reminiscent of the photocopier experiment we saw earlier, in which for small requests acceptance increased between 60 percent and 90 percent.

To test these three methods, the researchers asked sixty random passersby to look after a bicycle for ten minutes. The results were that 20 percent of people complied with the request when the DITF technique was used, 45 percent when the IP technique was used, and 60 percent when the "Why not?" technique was used. Statistically, the "Why not?" method outperformed the DITF technique and was as effective as IP.

This research does not allow us to know why the "Why not?" technique works so well in some situations, but Boster and his colleagues suggest that it is due to the persistence of the requestor. Repeated requests give the impression of urgency, which can make people feel guilty or attract their sympathy.

However, my favorite explanation has to do with cognitive dissonance. This has to do with the fact that we try to avoid inconsistencies in our thinking that cause us mental anguish. It is dissonant not to comply with a request after objections have actually been resolved. After all, if there is no reason not to do it, why not do it?

Although this experiment does not prove it, these techniques can be even more powerful when used together, especially as "Why not?" can be used in virtually any situation. The only drawback of "Why not?" is that it takes cunning to dispel objections. Even so, anticipating objections is a standard part of negotiation, so many of your responses can be prepared in advance. It may seem cheeky to keep asking "Why not?" when people refuse, but this experiment suggests that it can be an effective way to get your requests met.

CONCLUSION

We've come to the conclusion of this amazing journey. Now it is your duty to take it and develop it in your own way and for your own benefit.

We must never forget that words are powerful. After all, it was language in the first place that brought us to the top of the food chain. In today's world, it will still be our words that take us to the top of our personal food chain, in work and in life. Communication skills are more powerful than any other skill we can develop. Words inspire. Words sell. Words connect us. In fact, *Harvard Business Review* subscribers ranked communication skills as "the most important factor for an executive to be worthy of promotion," more important than ambition, education, hard work and even technical skills.

Tragically, communication skills are disappearing at an alarming rate. Whether or not this is due to the increased use of technology and the decrease in face-to-face interactions, research has shown that we are more narcissistic than at any time in human history. We spend an average of seven and a half hours a day looking at a screen, and our desire to get to know other people is dying out.

When people communicate, wonderful things happen. That is why the world needs more people who can lead others to action. We need leaders who can motivate, engage, influence and inspire. Most importantly, we need more people who know how to use the power of language patterns to bridge differences and connect with those around us.

Now that science has allowed us to glimpse how our words really affect the brains of those around us, we can be more effective catalysts for decision-making and begin to form more fruitful connections. You already have the tools. The only question now is, are you willing to use them?

The only way to make this work is to go out and practice. Let go of fear, doubt, and expectations, and just go out and have fun using the patterns you've learned. I assure you that as soon as you relax, you will start getting better results. When you practice, keep things simple and use sentences that are as short as possible.

Thank you for reading this book. You are certainly an intelligent person, and I like that. I don't know if you have begun to notice how good it is to possess this power.

I wish you much success!

www.ingramcontent.com/pod-product-compliance
Lightning Source LLC
Chambersburg PA
CBHW031438160426
43195CB00010BB/770

9798218037161